Contagious Love

by

Dan'l C. Markham

with vignettes by Nick Vujicic

Contagious Love™
Copyright © 2017 Dan'l C. Markham

Published by KeeptheFaith Publishing, a Division of BigOyo, LLC
2000 Mallory Lane, Suite 130-237
Franklin, Tennessee 37067
www.keepthefaith.com

All rights reserved. No portion of this book may be reproduced, stored in a retrieval system, or transmitted in any form or by any means—electronic, mechanical, photocopy, recording, scanning, or other—except for brief quotations in reviews or articles, without the prior written permission of the publisher.

All Scripture quotations are taken from the New King James Version (NKJV) unless otherwise noted. Scripture taken from the New King James Version. Copyright © 1982 by Thomas Nelson, Inc. Used by permission. All rights reserved.

Scripture quotations marked (NIV®) are taken from the HOLY BIBLE, NEW INTERNATIONAL VERSION ®. NIV®. Copyright © 1973, 1978, 1984, 2011 by Biblica, Inc.®. Used by permission. All rights reserved worldwide.

Scripture quotations marked NLT are taken from the *Holy Bible*, New Living Translation, copyright ©1996, 2004, 2007, 2013 by Tyndale House Foundation. Used by permission of Tyndale House Publishers, Inc., Carol Stream, Illinois 60188. All rights reserved.

Scripture quotations marked ESV are taken from the English Standard Version. No permission required.

Contagious Love™ is a trademark of BigOyo, LLC, used by permission.

Version KTF.003.2017.07

EDITIONS
ISBN: 978-0-9963005-4-4 (paperback)
ISBN: 978-0-9963005-5-1 (eBook)

Cover Design: Kim Russell/Wahoo Designs

Digital Design and Typeset: Telemachus Press, LLC
http://www.telemachuspress.com

A fuller theological treatment of Contagious Love is available under the title of The Lost Mandate from Father's Press at www.fatherspress.com or most Internet book retail locations.

Dan'l Markham is featured on KeepTheFaith Radio
America's #1 faith-based syndicated radio show

To experience Contagious Encouragement 24/7 visit
www.KeepTheFaith.com

Live radio, podcasts, events, articles, and first-person testimonies will help you discover the life-changing—and world-changing—faith to become the best you ever!

Dedication

While it was my mother, Mary Ann Markham, who taught me by her deeds to put compassion in action for others, I dedicate this book to Rick Eastin of Fresno, CA, as one who is representative of so many people affected by disability. That is, those who have not let their disability get in their way of fulfilling God's purposes for their lives. In fact, they have yielded their allegiance to Christ to let Him use them and their weaknesses for His glory. You people rock!

Acknowledgements

Among the people making this book a reality, none tower like Joni Eareckson Tada of Joni and Friends. Joni is a giant yet humble advocate for people affected by disability. I count it an honor to have served Joni and Friends and her for ten years.

Nick Vujicic of Life Without Limbs was gracious in providing his vignettes found at the conclusion of each chapter. Traveling with Nick for four years and seeing throngs of people flock to him hear about Jesus proves the very point of "God's power in weakness."

Thanks to Marie Kuck of Nathaniel's Hope—a leader in inspiring and equipping churches to serve those affected by disability, Professor Jeff McNair of Cal Baptist University who lives what he teaches, Lisa Copen of Rest Ministries, Debbie Kay of Hope for the Brokenhearted, Colleen Swindoll Thompson of Reframe Ministries and my spunky Shellie Nichol of Project Foster Care.

Then there are some churches who stand out in my mind who have been pioneers and leaders in disability ministry such as First Church of the Nazarene of Pasadena, Bethlehem Baptist of Minneapolis, Stonebriar Church of Frisco, TX, McLean Bible Church of McLean, VA and last but not least in my heart my Centerpoint Church of Simi Valley, CA.

Above all it is the hundreds of moms, dads and siblings of people affected by disability that push me forward in this great endeavor to whom I am so grateful.

Finally a huge thanks to my friend David Sams of Keep the Faith Radio who has kept the faith with me and millions of others.

"I have compassion for these people; they have already been with me three days and have nothing to eat. If I send them home hungry, they will collapse on the way, because some of them have come a long distance." - Mk. 8:2-3 (NIV)

When the Son of Man comes in His glory, and all the angels with Him, He will sit on His glorious throne. All the nations will be gathered before Him, and he will separate the people one from another as a shepherd separates the sheep from the goats… "Then the King will say to those on His right, 'Come, you who are blessed by my Father; take your inheritance, the kingdom prepared for you since the creation of the world. For I was hungry and you gave me something to eat, I was thirsty and you gave me something to drink, I was a stranger and you invited me in, I needed clothes and you clothed me, I was sick and you looked after me, I was in prison and you came to visit me.' "Then the righteous will answer Him, 'Lord, when did we see you hungry and feed you, or thirsty and give you something to drink? When did we see you a stranger and invite you in, or needing clothes and clothe you? When did we see you sick or in prison and go to visit you?' "The King will reply, 'Truly I tell you, whatever you did for one of the least of these brothers and sisters of mine, you did for me.' - Mtt. 25:31-40 (NIV)

Contagious Love...

"Wonderfully engaging, deeply challenging. An important read for anyone who desires to walk more fully in Christ's commands." - Bill Myers, bestselling author, *Eli and The God Hater*

"In *Contagious Love*, Dan'l Markham combines a clear eyed understanding of the Bible with a frank relating of personal experience… In the end you will have thought deeply about what it means to be 'real' in one's walk with God." - Professor Jeff McNair, California Baptist University

"Dan'l Markham has written a book that will challenge the presuppositions of every believer. If you're wondering what God meant when He said; 'Go into all the world and preach the gospel,' read this book. I strongly commend this seminal book to all believers." - Peter J. Iliyn, North American Director, Youth With A Mission

"*Contagious Love* is a much needed challenge to humbly and practically embrace the Biblical edict to reach out to those who are damaged, hurting, and less fortunate. This is particularly timely given the last 10 years of war, the wounded, widowed, unemployed, and economically destitute...and God's intent to use us as part of healing and restoration." - Major General Mastin M. Robeson, USMC (Ret)

Contents

Foreword

Before You Begin...

The other day I was reading a newsletter from my missionary friend, Margaret, who is serving among people with disabilities in Africa. When I read her second paragraph, I was moved to tears: "Cristina is disabled; a death sentence here in Tanzania. Her family discarded Cristina's body on the side of a dirt road to let fate decide what should happen next. Finding her unprotected, predatory men found Cristina and abused her…leaving her sitting in a pile of her own waste when missionaries finally found her."

Cristina's plight is not uncommon in the Majority World. The World Health Organization reports that there are over one billion people with disabilities and 80 percent of them live in desperate poverty. We can easily gloss over such a statistic, until we are stopped short by a story like Cristina's.

This is why I am so excited about my friend Dan'l Markham's new book, *Contagious Love.* Dan'l and I served as co-laborers in the global disability movement for many years through our work together at the Joni and Friends International Disability Center. His passion for the last and the "least of the brethren" was tireless. Time and again, I saw him go the extra mile and invest the extra effort to ensure that families affected by disability, whether here in the States or around the world, received help and hope from Christ.

Contagious Love is an insightful analysis of our Savior's words in Luke 14 to "Go out… find the disabled, lame and blind… and bring them in." Dan'l's research is a valuable contribution to the disability ministry movement and will be an encouragement to families and individuals affected by disability—consider it a primer of sorts.

Who should read this book? Pastors, disability ministry workers, and seminary and Bible college professors. The plight of children with disabilities like Cristina in Tanzania is too desperate, too urgent—we must mobilize the body of Christ to become part of the movement to advance Christ's Gospel into the darkest corners of the world… corners where people with disabilities are suffering from abuse, neglect, and hopelessness for the lack of hearing the Good News.

The book you hold in your hands will strike a match in your heart and ignite a passion to carry out the Luke 14 mandate here and abroad. So be blessed by the insights my friend Dan'l shares… and let me encourage you to pass this book on to your friends and co-laborers in the kingdom of Christ. Thank you for joining the movement, friend. For the sake of Cristina. For the sake of Jesus Christ.

Joni Eareckson Tada
Joni and Friends International Disability Center
Agoura Hills, California

Introduction

"Pressed Upon"

That something presses hard against my heart, again, as I write these words. Yours, too, I imagine.

It's actually not something but someone. That's God the Holy Spirit, pressing you to do something when you see pain and suffering. It is the woman with two kids and the cardboard sign at the Home Depot parking lot driveway, the suffering puppies on the television ad, or the story of hurt and loss being poured out in front of you by a loved one. You're pressed upon.

Even if you are not a Christian, you are created in the image of God and God's imprint causes you to care. In yielding to the pressure, into action, you will increasingly discover Him.

If you feel no pressing, God has drawn you to this book so He can share His heart with you for the least, the last, the lost, the shut in and the shut out—so you, too, might be pressed upon.

Yes, it's a little scary. But letting the pressure come upon your heart is God's push upon you to begin an astounding journey where you will discover life to its fullest—pain and purpose, suffering and stunning surprises, loss and love like you never knew it, loneliness and then tear popping joy from His tangible presence.

You are one who can see their faces, hear their cries and perceive enough that you can see beyond the smiles and laughter to the true need of a heart crying out.

They are crying out for you, looking for you, wondering if you will probe the behind the façade. And God is calling you.

As you step forward with compassion action, Jesus is actually walking by your side. You will see. You will know Him there, personally.

Read along. Come on along. It will not only be okay, it will be revolutionary for you and your world.

Give Him your hand.

Here we go.

- Chapter 1 -

Rock Your World

God sightings. You know what I'm talking about. Those wondrous moments when you are touched and moved by the compassionate unseen or seen hand of God, often when you least expect it—compassion connections.

Being stirred by an awe-inspiring, multi-tinted, sunset-bursting reflective light on a shimmering ocean, the delightful wonder of early dawn as birds of varied colors under the hand of an unseen conductor burst forth in welcoming the new day in a symphony of songs, a star lit sky under the backdrop of black as black while laying on your back on an open high desert looking up almost breathlessly, a sense of presence in a quiet time alone in your room or a prayer miraculously answered amidst joyful, spontaneous praise. God moments. God sightings. Compassion connections. We are designed to know God and experientially so.

Mother Teresa wrote, "We need to find God, and he cannot be found in noise and restlessness. God is the friend of silence. See how nature—trees, flowers, grass—grows in silence; see the stars, the moon and the sun, how they move in silence... We need silence to be able to touch souls."

The ancient Scottish Monk, Angus, when recording his thoughts and impressions after beholding a breathtaking, stunningly beautiful high valley in Scotland, called it a thin place. Thereafter, Celtic Christians came to identify thin places as physical spaces where heaven and earth touch, where God seems more readily present, more easily accessed, where the glory of God breaks into human existence. Angus meant it was a place where heaven and earth intersected or a place where one could sense that he or she was very close to heaven, to God. Jesus referred to thin places as "the Kingdom of God has come unto you"—where earth and heaven intersected under the presence and power of the King of the Universe.

Sometimes God sightings, compassion connections, thin places, are an awakening. Often in totally unexpected times, places and circumstances God personally reveals Himself. Sometimes He comes in the darkest of times. My friend, Jordan Lawhead, founder of YouInspire.org, tells of a God sighting, of his great moment of grace, of his great compassion connection, even though he was in a time of darkness and terror and seeming isolation from God. This occurred during a vicious vomiting cycle of doom in a sterile, cold hospital room brought on by a black box drug.

Jordan Lawhead, http://www.YouInspire.org, Nashville, TN

Get The Bucket!!!!

There are bumper stickers, T-shirts, and words from well-meaning strangers all saying, "God Loves You." But do we really feel that way?? What is it supposed to feel like? Like warm fuzziness from the sky or a cosmic sense of the infinite giving us a hug? I can only speak from my experience.

It was 2:00 a.m. and the nurse just came in to check my vital signs again. I laid my head back in frustration and fear after being woken up again to the sound of the machine's annoying bleeeeep, bleep, bleep to monitor my heart. Lying there in the glow of the instruments I had a very honest moment with God. This was my darkest moment in my life. I was just told I had 3 to 6 months to live and that stage 4 Melanoma was raging like a wildfire inside my body. The only option I had was that I was just given a black box warning (it can kill you) drug called interluken that the docs said only had a 5% chance of working. Staring at the ceiling like I was looking into the face of God, I was the most truthful I had ever been and with these simple words I said, "I don't really feel like you love me." It was like a flash of lightning ran through my body that second after I finished those words. It wasn't the immediate sense of love I was hoping for, it was the moment we all face when we're about to barf and we get that chill down our spine and the drop in our stomach and our eyes get real big and we yell, "GET THE BUCKET!!!"

My dad was sleeping in a recliner chair next to me and, like the waking of an old English sheep dog, he jumped up with surprise and disorientation, "Huh? What?? Oh!!!." He grabs the blue bucket just in time for me to lose it. The darkest moment I was talking about just got a little more dark… After I was done, I sat back and my father grabbed a warm washcloth and wiped my face, my forehead, and my chin. All without words he held the bucket for me in the darkness. I couldn't help but see the miracle that just happened before my eyes. The miracle was the moment I realized the love of God isn't just a fuzzy feeling from the sky, but the people in our lives who hold the bucket in our darkest moments. The human hands and heart right there in the room with me were doing what they were designed to be doing; that love has to come from somewhere. That love has to have a source. We are all the earthly expressers of the love of God and I dare to say even if we don't believe in God we can show

His love. The historical figure of Jesus Christ was the purest form of the embodiment of God's love sent to hold the bucket for all of humanity in our sickness, darkness, and shame. To wipe our face, our forehead, and our chin with human hands and a heart with a lasting message of mercy and grace for anyone who might receive His love.

It was in 2008 when I was diagnosed, and I am beyond grateful to be healthy and on the other side of those dark times.

Once I began to open my eyes and look for the love of God in other people, it changed the way I see His love. Everyday my prayer is that my hands and heart might be His hands and heart, with a bucket that would be ready for anybody who might need it.

His dad was his compassion connector. You can be one, too—in simple acts of kindness and in powerful, amazing ways.

The book you hold in your hands is about God showing up in weakness and suffering—yours or walking with others in theirs—as He compassionately accompanies us through suffering rather than instantaneously taking it away, which He could do and sometimes does do.

This book, in part, is about my journey with God through and because of my suffering…and triumphantly out the other side because of His great compassion and his use of others in extending His compassion

During the darkest hours of my life, I had my first 'midnight of my soul' God sightings as I would sit on a stump in a small forest and just pour out my heart in conversation to Him. I just talked with

Him and in doing so became aware of His presence in my suffering.

And make no mistake about it. Compassion is hard work, and at times gut wrenching, with various kinds of buckets for the vomit of life on earth.

In the teaching of Christ and the entire New Testament compassion IS NOT primarily a feeling. The Bible does not know compassion apart from action. It is often hard work on behalf of God for others.

This book is also about a fledgling worldwide movement of God, which has been conceived out of the intersection of suffering and heaven—a movement that invites dreamers of the day. You'll learn about the dangerous dreamers of the day in just a few pages.

Dreamers of the Day

Rocker Ozzy Osborne, capturing the same emotions and desires of John Lennon in his words from *Imagine*, wrote these lyrics in his popular song *Dreamer*:

> *If only we could all just find serenity*
> *It would be nice if we could live as one*
> *When will all this anger, Hate*
> *and bigotry… Be gone?*
>
> *I'm just a dreamer*
> *I dream my life away*
> *Today*

I'm just a dreamer
Who dreams of better days
Okay
I'm just a dreamer
Who's searching for the way

Made in the image of God all humans are dreamers. Some of the humans of grand value to us are men and women of extreme vision, mega dreamers. These are people who will stop at nothing less than to transform their home, their neighborhood, their community, their culture, their school, their world whether their culture or world be as small as their family or larger than the earth itself. These aren't 'hope-ers,' but dreamers.

Dreamers imagine the impossible as possible. They move beyond the dream, the vision. They do something about it, relentlessly so, often compelled, even obsessed and sometimes not knowing why. It just is. That is our compassionate, sovereign God of providential care moving through us.

I pray that God will ignite your heart along with other dreamers and potential dreamers—all who travel these pages who want to see the darkest places in the world turned into marvelous light, whether they are in a slum in Bangkok or the bedroom of a suburban home in Dallas.

History is full of such dreamers who God used to change the world.

God chose to use flawed human beings, but flawed human beings with motivation, vision, passion, and a whole lot of elbow grease.

After God gives us a dream, He calls us to work. It's tough work. But it's the preeminent work, the most rewarding work. It's for man on behalf of God.

Here's a news flash. You don't have to wish for a movement of God or go back in time. God is always on the move—forward. This book is a surefire road map to getting on a movement of the Holy Spirit. Albeit in its fledgling years, this movement is sure to build and bloom until the revival of the Holy Spirit spills out of hearts touched by God, the Holy Spirit, across cities, lands, and the world itself in radical witness for Christ through (apparent) weakness.

I'm going to share secrets from a mystical world that has mind bending suffering in conjunction with surprising, tear dropping joy—a place where you can catch a Jesus-infused dream, which to this day has been obscured from view and sidelined by church and society.

It's just a matter of letting God radicalize your heart—to be radically crazy like Jesus (Mk. 3:20-21). Of course He wasn't 'crazy' crazy, but he had been so radicalized by the worldview of His Father and by power of the Holy Spirit [1] that he saw the world through a new lens, knowing in time things were never going to be the same. So crazy with the love and the power of God that His enemies accused Him of being demon possessed. He was possessed all right—by the Holy Spirit. The years of his carpentry life in Nazareth were over. He was now heaven bent on manifesting and launching the Kingdom of Heaven on earth, elsewhere called the Kingdom of God.

---

[1] Luke 3:21-4:1, 4:14-22.

If you finish this book and are affected by it and decide to do something about the truth of the words of Jesus expressed in this book, I suspect you will become radicalized by Jesus to bring powerful liberating change in a world of desperate needs—your world. You may just be become a crazy radical like Jesus. I'm so excited for you.

Along the way, as you travel the pages of *Contagious Love,* my life story will emerge like a bobbing log in a river's current, as a sort of backdrop to philosophical and religious problems and troubling questions—the ones Jesus spoke about and the ones we all face today. I believe the journey of this weathered log, along with the Scriptures herein, will bring more than a ray of hope to you that there is a real God, who is Jesus, who redeems all of life's positives and negatives—the good, the bad, and the ugly—and turns them for good—a compassionate God who shows up. Indeed, in the midst of my darkness, He flooded my place with light. In my weakness He distributed beautiful, disturbing power, just like He will do for you, whether you are a Christ follower or not.

Young prophetic [2] preachers like Pastor Francis Chan in his call to radical Christian faith through his book *Crazy Love: Overwhelmed by a Relentless God,* and Pastor Jason Walls, author of *Radical: Taking Back Your Faith from the American Dream,* are fostering a fledgling movement of Millenials, X-Gens and even Busters and Boomers who are becoming dreamers with radical world changing faith.

---

[2] I use the term prophetic here not in the sense of foretelling but forth-telling, i.e. to bring a counter culture, radical message. It is radical because it is rooted in the Biblical text and contrary to the prevailing culture, even the prevailing Christian culture.

Pastor Mike Barrett, another young prophetic preacher from Lincoln City, Oregon, writing in *Christianity Today,* [3] lets us know that radical faith, as this book reveals, comes from the roots of Christianity, yes from Christ Himself:

> *Radical, in its origins, really means to be rooted. The idea behind the word is to be so grounded, so deeply rooted in a lifestyle direction that one stands against the social and cultural currents that tear others away from that same path. It's not so much forcing a change, of course, but returning oneself and others to an originally intended path. By this definition, classic radicalism is found in the lives of many historical figures, people who stood up for human rights and religious reform. Today, anyone who adheres to the person and teachings of Christ in the midst of runaway humanism and hedonism is, by definition, a radical. It's essentially building your house on a rock that doesn't get torn down in cultural storms. So becoming a true* radical *is to return oneself and others to a sacred path, and to stand against modernity's eroding influences… So, on a night when the outside world pretends to care less, I try to take that bittersweet pill of old-fashioned repentance, hoping to wake up tomorrow morning infected again by the blood of Christ, diseased and unable to extricate myself from His grip. I'm compelled to be a true radical—to be truly rooted—right here in my small hometown, through my little local church, regardless of the cost or how long it takes.*

So radical Christianity is people with true, raw, unabashed Biblical faith in Christ and His word; people who take Christ and His word at face value and decide to live it accordingly.

---

[3] Feb. 2009 "Searching for Radical Faith"

Again, compassion is not a feeling. It is a radical commitment to action and for standing tall for what's right against all else, if necessary. People who feel compassion and do nothing about it are not compassionate AT ALL.

We're talking about living an amazing life for God from your kitchen, your workshop, your business, your workplace, your Sunday school room, your home fellowship, your school or university, your women's circle, your golf buddies, your Starbucks hangers on, your football game beer buddies, your baseball team, your kids' carpool, your classmates.

Shake It Up

Whether we know it, we all need to experience Christianity in its true, gutsy, no-apologies raw state, reflected in the kind of life Jesus lived. A half-baked, lukewarm Christianity is, well it's what Jesus said was nothing but 'spit.'[4] Ergo, we need Jesus in His raw reality. Otherwise Jesus will be relegated in our minds and hearts and in society to just one of many great people in history. And then Christianity will be just another religion, even more marginalized than it already is, especially in Western culture. Jesus deserves better representatives than the lukewarm kind. Spit is uncool. Redeeming fervor is hot!

This book and the truths it brings forth will bring you raw, authentic Christianity as I believe Jesus intended. If you will allow it, it will radically change you. It will take on the tough dilemmas of suffering, evil, and death. It will tackle the dark side of religion, yes Christian religion, such as pride, self-righteousness, discrimination, and self-absorption. I pray the raw beauty of the simplicity that is in

---

[4] Revelations 3:16. The literal word used in the Bible's original language is "vomit" or "spit."

Christ-centered truth will be unveiled to you as you read. This, I pray, resulting in you bringing life changing power into your personal world, and perhaps the worlds of others, as a compassion connector of *Contagious Love.*

> *The paradox is when you draw near to the places and people of suffering with the wonders of Jesus's words, His example and His empowering presence. You will become addicted to the discovery of Him, His presence, and what he does through you in transforming places of darkness. You will be amazed at finding Him in the face of the sufferers of the world as in turn your personal, hidden dark places are then transformed by them.*

Sounds crazy, ehhh? Crazy wonderful!

This journey involves one billion people living along and on the side streets of Amsterdam, the huts of Africa, the hovels of Central America, and the teeming ghettos of India as well as the clean yet emotionally and spiritually sterile "modern" care facilities in western countries.

More importantly, our journey will take you into a little known three month trek with Jesus. This just before His crucifixion, when He fled from Jerusalem's harassing, harping, religious zealots, whose judgmental and haughty religion did not relate to the common man nor to Jesus, nor especially to the poor and people affected by disabilities. Beginning in Luke Chapter 13, this is a trip that took Him eastward into the relative peace of the simple countryside on the other side of the Jordan River—a little known obscure province in the vast Roman Empire known as Perea. Jesus, you'll learn, delights in working in little, obscure places and through seemingly insignificant people.

Yes, what these pages seek out is the best in you and God's best for you. It is sounding the alarm to awaken that thing inside you that desires genuineness and significance.

T. E. Lawrence, the Lawrence of Arabia guy wrote, "All men dream, but not equally. Those who dream by night in the dusty recesses of their minds, wake in the day to find that it was vanity: but the dreamers of the day are dangerous men, for they may act on their dreams with open eyes, to make them possible."

So, first and foremost, God is looking for visionaries, the "dreamers of the day," the dangerous kind. Let's get crazy dangerous in our dreaming.

Jesus, the ultimate dream maker, had a vision of the Kingdom of God, which was partly described in his famous Sermon on the Mount. [7] He could see it, and He explained it in detail throughout the Gospels. He constantly talked about it. He lived it and modeled it. He launched it, bringing it into a darkened world. [5] He willingly and knowingly gave the ultimate sacrifice for it. Jesus didn't just command us to preach and live the Gospel, He exhorted us to preach and live the Gospel *of the Kingdom*, as He did as a compassion connector.

Jesus wants you and me to catch His Kingdom dream; a vision of how the world should be; where social, economic, and spiritual 'justice rolls like a river.' [6] The kind of place that John Lennon hoped for, and Martin Luther King not only dreamed of, but

---

[5] Lk. 10:9,11; 11:20

[6] Amos 5:24

worked to make happen and died for. This Kingdom of God is coming to pass, and it will one day fully come to pass.

Something is stirring in Christ's followers, an emerging worldwide movement based upon what is increasingly being referred to as the Luke 14 Mandate. As a mandate from Jesus, it must be heeded. It involves the most passionate, compassionate and aggressive call to the proclamation of the Good News of the Kingdom in the New Testament and thus to our world, His world. This is a kind of Good News that even non-Christ followers understand and admire.

> *Then He also said to him who invited Him, 'When you give a dinner or a supper, do not ask your friends, your brothers, your relatives, nor rich neighbors, lest they also invite you back, and you be repaid. But when you give a feast, invite the poor, the maimed, the lame, the blind. And you will be blessed, because they cannot repay you; for you shall be repaid at the resurrection of the just'... So that servant came and reported these things to his master. Then the master of the house, being angry, said to his servant, "Go out quickly into the streets and lanes of the city, and bring in here the poor and the maimed and the lame and the blind." And the servant said, "Master, it is done as you commanded, and still there is room." Then the master said to the servant, "Go out into the highways and hedges, and compel them to come in, that my house may be filled..."* (Lk. 14:12-14, 21-24)

Did you catch the force of such words as *angry, quickly* and *compel*? Watch out now. If you take this seriously you will be thought of as crazy. Why would you waste your time on those the world rejects and ignores, the marginalized...? Yes, the very ones Jesus was preoccupied with.

It is a dream culminating in the end of ages at *The* Great Banquet Feast, at a time when the least and the last, the shut-in and the shut-out, the poor and those affected by disabilities will indeed have their rightful place in God's house, in God's Church, in God's world, in God's economy, in the Kingdom of God, at His supper table of fellowship. This is a time when the evil kingdoms of this world and ugly religious attitudes are turned on their heads—completely—as they become the Kingdom of our Christ.[7]

My friend, Bill Goodrich, is such a dreamer of the day, fostering a movement for every church in the United States to adopt a long-term care facility in their neighborhood.[8] And it's happening!

While still in its initial stages, these compassionate "dream makers of a different kind" are forerunners of an unanticipated fledgling worldwide movement. This movement is touching the largest grouping of people on earth—1 billion people with a disability[9]—who are the richest in faith according to James, the half-brother of Jesus (Jam. 2:5). The ministry in this movement is at a spiritual address where the Apostle Matthew declared Christ himself could be found, ministered to, and experienced—in the presence of the poor, the prisoner, the stranger, yes those with disabilities. (Mtt. 25)

You, your family, your church and your generation have the rare opportunity to be part of the legacy of history's company of Godly dream makers and to be part of a dream making, visionary movement. In the natural it is probably the last place your church or you would want to go. It is definitely a walk into the "uncomfortable zone."

---

[7] Rev. 11:15

[8] www.godcaresministry.com

[9] Source: Disability Funders Network

But, it is a place of innumerable compassion connections, and thus, God sightings.

Let's get crazy. Be dreamers of the day, and discover God's presence and power in the most unlikely of places!

Chapter 1
Nick's Note

Yea mate, that's an awesome thing to consider. God gives dreams to us for us to fulfill for Him.

The God who fills eternity, all the earth and the heavens, who knows all things at all times instantaneously, who scattered abroad the universe with a wave of his creative hand, has decided it is in His interest and ours to give us a vision of something birthed in the heart of the divine, transferred to our hearts for us and our generation to fulfill.

My friend Dan'l is really onto something here. I'm on board completely. If you want to be a world changer, whether in your neighborhood, your school, your circle of friends, your church or the globe, I say join us…get on board.

When I was little, my parents, doctors, and teachers could not see that I would be an evangelist who traveled the world. That's because my dream wasn't Nick V's dream. It was God's dream for me. And once you discover God's dream for you—whether big or small in the eyes of man—no obstacle can stop you if every day you take a step in the direction of your dream, no matter the resistance, no matter how many times you stumble or fall. Get up and get with it every day.

I see you in the arenas, stadiums, churches, universities, schools, and city streets around the United States and the world. God created you with a yearning for the Divine. Black, white, brown, or in between; old, young, or in the middle; able bodied or with a disability; male or female, your heart yearns to take hold of the hope of the message of the Good News. The hope that is being realized in movements such as the spiritual and social justice movements for and of the people this book elevates—the poor, those affected by disability, the outcast, the weak, the last, the lost, the least, the shut in and the shut out.

Yea, I see it every day in your eyes. You want a better world and you want to make a difference.

Life is short. Yet it can be very, very good if we begin setting our eyes upon the horizon of God-given dreams and then do something about it…relentlessly.

- Chapter Two -

No Immunity

It began in the fall of 1994, upon my return from my third short-term mission in three years into the heart of Russia. It was enormously exciting and joyful to come back to my wife, three daughters, and my vibrant church, which was part of my childhood Pacific Coast fishing village.

My roots run deep in the very southwestern corner of the State of Washington where the Columbia River, flowing through temperate rain forests of the Pacific Northwest, meets the Pacific Ocean. It was here, after crossing the Oregon Trail, my great grandfather, Dan Markham, a Civil War veteran, pioneered in the 1870s. As a charter member and lay preacher of the Methodist Church in Ilwaco, Washington, Town Marshall, and a civic leader, my great grandfather and later my grandfather, who worked the rough and tumble boom and bust cycles of the salmon fishing industry, left quite a legacy for me. My mom, Mary Ann, an RN, was a modern day Florence Nightingale. Dad, Ernie Markham, was a World War II vet who everyone loved. He was laughter with a capital L. I had the best of lives—realizing my dreams of raising a family in this

Tom Sawyer-like town—hunting, fishing and working on the waterfront from the time I was a runt.

I was blessed beyond measure to see my dream come true as Christ used me to make a major kingdom impact in my hometown area, pioneering a growing evangelical church, and even being elected to the community's highest elected position, County Commissioner.

My mission trips to Russia were glorious, seeing God do so many wondrous things after the Iron Curtain fell as the Gospel of Christ was being proclaimed with power. Hundreds came to Christ as the miraculous accompanied my preaching and teaching ministry. As part of a 'Youth With A Mission' training team, scores of Russian-born missionaries and future pastors were trained to change the spiritual landscape of their beloved nation. As I called back to my church during those weeks, the church's vision for their local community and the world expanded.

Years of sacrifice and hard work coupled with God's grace were culminating in fruitfulness and success as my fondest dreams were coming to pass. Life couldn't be better.

Except…except little did I know as I stepped off my plane in Portland, Oregon, that what awaited me was going to be a nightmare that only the enemy of our souls could devise. My dream realized was about to be shattered, and I would soon be devastated by defeat on every front.

Conversely, I had no way of knowing that the coming obliteration of my life and soul would eventually be the seed that would germinate into an even greater fulfillment of a God-given dream larger than my mind or heart would allow.

Upon my return home, the elders of my church quickly let me know that something was amiss with my wife in regards to her personal ministry to a troubled person in our community. What started as ministry to a woman, who supposedly came to seek counsel from me regarding her homosexuality, turned into a bonding and affection between my wife and her, which was disturbing to family, friends, and church members.

"What is this?" I asked with bewilderment. Surely, everyone must be misreading what was going on. But reality defeated my denial. Upon seeing that the relationship between the two was unhealthy, I challenged my wife to end this 'ministry' relationship. I was rebuffed.

I was stunned into an emotional stupor and mind-bending disbelief. This couldn't be happening.

Soon I was informed by my wife that she wanted to continue her relationship with this woman, this after 23 years of marriage—including six years of secular and Bible college, three children, and fifteen years in pastoral ministry. I was dumbfounded, shell shocked.

Two years followed with tormenting emotional, physical, mental and economic devastation.

Loss of self-esteem accompanied by self-doubt stretched my faith to the breaking point. I cried out again and again, "God, you are a

God of love. Why are you allowing this? Or are you inflicting it upon me? Why? What have I done to deserve this? Where are you? Stop this terrifying nightmare! Please, God, help me!" Nothing in my theological training had prepared me for such suffering.

I prayed in desperation, again and again, as I uncontrollably wept with a depth of wrenching and unrelenting grief and sorrow, which pulled my guts up through my heart. One such excruciating grieving spell went on for two hours, as I laid in the fetal position in a bath of tears, in my car in the parking lot of the Lloyd Center Mall in Portland, Oregon. This as Sarah and Angela, my two oldest girls, did their Christmas shopping.

The pain was unrelenting, and sleep was impossible except when brought on by two glasses of wine and a sleep-aid. [10] The idea of waking up was terrifying, which made falling asleep a mixture of blessing and curse. I was in grave trouble. Each and every day was unbearable as I stumbled on in my dark haze of depression, painfully putting one plodding foot in front of the other.

There were other losses in addition to the unimaginable bereavement over the loss of my marriage. There was the loss of my pastoral calling and my church, which meant more to me than words can express. The church didn't ask me to step down. I was just too much of an emotional wreck to lead, and thus resigned, with no sense of how I would care for my soon to be ex-wife and children.

---

[10] This is not something I recommend. Yet it demonstrates what desperate shape I was in. After a few months I sought professional medical help for my depression and sleep deprivation. The depression is gone, but the sleep deprivation has been unrelenting for 20 years, a lingering reminder of the midnight of my soul.

There were financial and social losses, even to the point of being ostracized by some friends, colleagues, and family in Christ. False rumors turned vicious. "He had an affair with the church secretary." "He was secretly a wife abuser." The wagging finger was pointed at the fallen pastor, community leader, and former county commissioner.

Others stood by me, just being there for me, which meant everything. They walked with me in my pain. Their compassion was medicine to my soul.

Like a ball rolling ever so slowly from port to starboard on a lumbering ship, I laboriously see-sawed between true and false guilt as I tried to figure out my culpability in this life altering experience.[11]

I became the classic basket case. I slid down an unforgiving, ever darkening slope, entering the misty and terrifying world of grim, clinical-like depression. I was in pain everywhere. As I trudged along, I somehow managed during this time to work and provide for my daughters and soon to be ex-wife.

Simply put, on a scale of 1–10, I was at a negative 5.

Yet, fifteen years later, I found myself in a loving, caring church, totally blessed and privileged to be remarried, and the father of not

---

[11] By the way, I have no ill will toward my ex-wife. She had to have been enduring a secret, lonely world of incredible emotional pain and confusion to take the path she took. Regretfully, I learned that I too, had some responsibility for this loss. I was often too busy with ministry to see the secret pains my wife had been living with for years, all the while thinking I was not one of those pastors who would fail to meet his wife's needs. She re-married, to her former high school sweetheart, who seems to be a good man.

only three, but seven daughters. Yes…seven as in four plus three. Six grandkids, too! Two boys!

I also had the incredible honor of being a managing director of a ministry that addresses suffering in the name of Christ on a global scale, heading up ministry programs that were reaching thousands for Christ annually around the world.

This was fulfilling an identical vision in the mind's eye of three different, unrelated people, who shared with me on three different occasions, separated by years and locations, what they believe God showed them about my future. Once, after being born again, while in the Jesus People Movement, from a former Captain in the US Air Force. Again during the early years in church ministry by someone whose name I can't remember. And then, finally, in my early forties when in pastoral ministry from a fellow pastor I received an identical message for me.

Each person quoted Jeremiah 1:4-10 stating that the Lord had impressed upon them I would be a leader in a world reaching Christian movement. It sounded so incredible, so impossible, and so loaded with potential head swelling words, that I just nodded kindly and put it all on the proverbial shelf. How could a simple and broken country pastor from an out-of-the-way fishing village, who graduated from a bible college that later went down in flames of controversy, come to realize such mind-boggling things? Just not possible. Unless…and only unless…it was God, the Great Compassion Connector.

So God took this totally broken down, former senior pastor, this emotionally and spiritually crippled man, through a series of employment scenarios. During which I felt totally lost from God's calling, all in order to teach me (unbeknownst to me at the time) about Himself and me, and to impart skills and illuminate talents, which would result in me being recommended for a position at the worldwide ministry of Joni and Friends. I was being carried by God, but didn't see it until years later. Then, six-and-one-half years after being Director of U.S. Field Services at Joni and Friends, I was, to my surprise, promoted to oversee all national programs and an international outreach program—Wheels for the World—through which entire communities and nations were being affected by the Gospel—specifically the Luke 14 Mandate.

So it was in the aftermath of the destruction of my first dream—to make a kingdom impact on my hometown community and to raise a Godly family—that God eventually brought these 'words from the Lord' to pass, words which I had viewed with considerable skepticism, given my circumstances. Simply amazing! God's grace and ways are so incredible. He truly transforms ashes into beauty and mourning into joy. It seems to me, more often than not, there are certain kinds of beauty and joy, which can only come about through ashes and mourning. All because of compassion connections.

Today, given the awesome redemptive nature of a loving Savior, I can even joke about that hellish season of my life, commenting about my clinical-like depression that "the only thing I missed was the clinic." It's okay. You can laugh. LOL already!

So, I learned the hard way, like so many others, that no one is immune from suffering. Yet I also learned that those who suffer in this earthly existence can become the beneficiaries of the redemptive, life transforming nature of God. That is, gaining some of the sought after prize described by the Apostle Paul, which is to know Christ more intimately (Phil. 3:10), because of suffering, not in spite of it.

Suffering indeed brings polarizing influences into our lives—mourning and consolation, ashes and beauty, even praise in place of heaviness, rejection of God or greater intimacy with His Son. It comes in doses of every size—from hurtful, to painful, to crushing.

By shutting out or being in denial about suffering, or at least by doing our best to protect ourselves from it, we also lose out on many aspects of meaningful, godly, Holy Spirit produced joy, Christ-like beauty, divine consolation, and eternal usefulness.

In the past I did everything and anything to avoid pain and suffering. Truth be known, there is still a part of me (probably a larger part than my ego is willing to admit) that hopes severe suffering will not again be a part of my life experience. I still have a hard time fully engaging in Paul's prayer in Philippians 3:10, *"That I might know him, the power of this resurrection and the fellowship of His suffering.*[12]*"* Really? I get the praying for power, but suffering? I've learned to accept suffering as ordained or allowed by God for His greater good in me and through me. But praying for it? Well, I just can't fully get that in my 'getter.'

The world of disability ministry has suffering as its common and constant companion. It is enormous, as one billion people worldwide have disabilities according to the World Health Organization. It is also a world of contrasts—incredible times of joy-filled service in Christ, to and from others, and yet breathtaking,

---

[12] Underlining is mine.

sometimes intellectually and emotionally staggering suffering. This suffering, then coupled with stupefying consternation, usually ends in the big "Why?" questions at God, who can seem in some of those times to be distant, even withdrawn. But He is not. He is actually present in suffering. He is looking for others to be like Christ, His son, that is, looking for Christ-ians to be compassion connectors between humans and the divine.

We learn from God's Word that no matter how mind-boggling things may be, He is in control, seeing and knowing all that is happening to our world and to us. That, too, can be perplexing, frustrating, and angering. Yea, I got mad at God. Several times. He's got big shoulders. He can handle it. He can handle your frustration and anger, too.

Back in the 1990s, when going through the midnight of my soul as depression—with resulting pain racking my body and mind like unceasing breakers crashing on the jagged, eroding shore of heart and mind—a counselor gave me some advice. He said, "Dan'l embrace your suffering like embracing a bulldozer as it is slowly crushing your body." There was no way I could compute that mental picture. It didn't work in my neat and tidy theological world, one in which God would bring or allow serious suffering only if I was in some sort of unrepentant state of soul or needing discipline. The only other option was that He was *allowing* into my life this hell devised affliction; allowing as in deference to causing. It couldn't have been part of His will for my life. Right?

Due to God's sovereign providential care, it is possible in times of suffering to live in two seemingly opposing states at the same time. It's like imagining our legs are caught in the alligator jaws of pain, while at the same time our hearts and spirits are able to lay in comfort against that eternal breast that encased the heart broken for us all.

This heavy equipment analogy would have been much easier for me during my season of suffering if my counselor friend would have told me to embrace Christ instead of the bulldozer. He should have told me, "Christ will be your answer."

Christ will walk hand in hand with you through it. *But when you are tempted, he will also provide a way out so that you can endure it."*[13] NIV) Words and counseling will not be so much your answer as Christ Himself will be the answer. This is how to walk through life, triumphant in our trials. In fact, Christ is the way and the way-maker through valleys of sorrow and suffering and atop the mountains of victory and rejoicing.

It sounds trite and is no doubt overused: "Christ is the answer." This isn't as much an intellectual or theological thought or revelatory statement as it is something experienced in and with Christ. That is, it is simply holding on to our relationship with Christ, holding on to Christ himself; not by wrestling with theology or doctrine, or even Godly counsel, but embracing him as we go through it all. It is this embracing that results in the eventual transforming victory of Christ being realized in us.

Trust me. Hold onto Christ. It will make more sense as we move along. Christianity, Christian spiritual life, was meant to not only be in the mind philosophically and intellectually, but to be experienced—actually experienced. It's living—not letter only.

---

[13] I Co. 10:13, NIV.

Suffering isn't outside of God's control. In fact, it is one of His primary tools of choice in forming Christ in us. As the Apostle Paul clearly understood, simultaneously living in this place of seemingly opposing realms of power and suffering is a union and a process, instead of a completed project on this side of heaven. Neither is it a dualistic state of mind or soul.

Power and suffering were instruments in God's loving hands, using them to mold and make Paul into who He was and was yet to become in Christ Jesus.

Jesus is the prototype. We are the type. What was the Father's will for him is the Father's will for us. This is why Paul could teach us on the blessed results of suffering as recorded in Romans Chapter 5. [14] He knew firsthand the good stuff that suffering produced. Not only was he not ashamed of suffering, he embraced it, as did Christ. He had tasted its sweet fruits. He boasted in his suffering. Was he crazy? Yes, crazy like Jesus.

> *Therefore, most gladly I will rather boast in my infirmities that the power of Christ may rest upon me. Therefore, I take pleasure in infirmities, in reproaches, in needs, in persecutions, in distresses, for Christ's sake. For when I am weak, then I am strong.* - II Cor. 12:9-10

Philippians 1:29 reads, *For to you it has been granted on behalf of Christ, not only to believe in Him, but also to suffer for His sake.*

There is a 'Gospel light' being preached from pulpits today that says "just come to Jesus and you will have a life of roses," and if you don't, it's your fault. You don't have enough faith. The actual

---

[14] Romans 5:3-5

Gospel Jesus and Paul preached and lived was one of sacrifice for God and others, coupled with the intimacy of God through suffering and His accompanying provisions, peace, power and joy.

As Christians, especially in western civilization, we are pretty certain God wants to bless us with peace, joy, and stuff. For the most part we are not a people prepared for suffering. Not from media and not from pulpits. We are, more often than not, shocked into bewilderment when suffering comes our way. Too many people have crashed and burned mentally, emotionally, and spiritually due to a lack of biblical understanding regarding suffering.

Due to the Fall of mankind, suffering came into reality. Since the Fall of mankind into sin, suffering has been used by God to get our attention and to transform us into the image and likeness of Christ. And it works.

As my counselor advised, we can embrace suffering, but better yet, we can accept our suffering when it comes, and if it remains can overcome it by embracing Christ at the same time. Then, and only then, with Christ in us and us in Christ, comes *the* answer. He truly is *the* answer—Christ, not words or explanations, but Christ. He Himself marries suffering and joy into a union for His glory for us and in us. He pioneered this fiery trail to enable us to live in this seemingly impossible oxymoronic relationship of suffering and joy.

No immunity from suffering, my friends. Yet no reason to not experience a joy filled life in Christ.

So, may your journey be one of discovery in which the Holy Spirit graces you with a biblical kind of personal knowledge, an experiential knowledge, which leads to an understanding of the great questions and the great life transforming benefits of compassionate sacrifice and suffering; sacrificing and suffering for yourself, for the Church, and for a dying and decaying world, that they and you might experience the touch of God. It is then the world will truly be able to relate to you as a Christ follower. Over 1.4 billion people live in poverty and suffering [15] worldwide, including 15.1 percent of people in the U.S. or 47,414,000 Americans.

Human beings brought sin, and its suffering affects upon us all, and we upon ourselves. Consequently, God has chosen human beings to do something about it. It's called compassion, that is, compassion the verb. It's action not feelings, compassion connecting, albeit feelings do sometimes prompt us to action and accompany our actions.

So bring it on!

Pray with me, as followers of Jesus, to tap into God's plan and power to utilize weaknesses (yours, mine, and others). So that He will fulfill His purposes in this generation through those audacious enough to believe He truly desires to use the weak in personally transforming our places of darkness and myriads of such places into His glorious light.

Chapter Two
Nick's Note

My mom and dad and I know about the reality of no immunity from suffering.

---

[15] www.trickleup.org

While Mom and Dad always trusted Jesus, the shock of me being born healthy, yet with no arms or legs, hit them like a freight train.

The anguish and anxiety must have been almost overwhelming, especially at first.

I had no choice about suffering. I was born facing it, permanently.

We all have choices about suffering. You can choose to enter the world of suffering by finding Jesus in the place of the poor and those affected by disability, or you can retreat to your unfulfilling comfort zone.

In spite of it all Mom, Dad and I have found a life full of hope, joy and fulfillment because Jesus makes all the difference.

Once I accepted who I was in God, created by God for His purposes, He gave me a dream of reaching the world with the hope of the Gospel.

Life is great!

- Chapter Three -

The Unlikely

You are probably one of the unlikely.

> *Jesus said to them, "My food is to do the will of Him who sent Me, and to finish His work. Do you not say, 'There are still four months and then comes the harvest'? Behold, I say to you, lift up your eyes and look at the fields, for they are already white for harvest! And He who reaps receives wages, and gathers fruit for eternal life, that both He who sows and He who reaps may rejoice together.* - Jn. 4:34-36, NKJV

> *2 Then He said to them, "The harvest truly is great, but the laborers are few; therefore pray the Lord of the harvest to send out laborers into His harvest. 3 Go your way; behold, I send you out as lambs among wolves…9 And heal the sick there, and say to them, 'The Kingdom of God has come near to you.'* - Lk. 10:2-3, 9

It is in these seminal Great Commission passages Jesus gives us a sneak preview of what I call The Lost Mandate—Luke 14:12-24. These texts, tied with Luke 14:12-24, tell us what is still yet to come for the Church and for you and me in fulfilling the Great Commission, in being pioneers and prophets of His Kingdom, sharing principles and power with a world of desperate need.

We need many more *laborers* to *finish His work*. But we need to know what work needs to be completed in its entirety and who are the laborers. Certainly it is to bring the Gospel to all nations (ethnic groups). [16] In the classic sense these four texts listed in the footnote make up the Great Commission. Yet further investigation into God's Word reveals a more detailed picture of what and who are included in the Great Commission. Those who are to bring forth the Kingdom of God, which is indeed the end game in Christ's mind, and His glorious intentions with us and through us for others.

In the fourth chapter of John, the people whom Jesus was referring to and looking upon—*Behold, I say to you, lift up your eyes and look at the fields, for they are already white for harvest!* (Jn. 4:35b)—were a foretelling of sorts of how and by whom that *work* would be finished—at least in part. In John Chapter Four it was the uneducated, unsophisticated and unrefined apostles, AND it was the woman at the well returning with her Samaritan neighbors (4:28-30) to come and see a man she thought might very well indeed be the Messiah! As Jesus was looking at this flock of people moving across the Samaritan sea of ripening grain fields, He was speaking about the *unlikely*. They and millions like them were the harvest to be reaped. Some will be laborers for the owner of the fields to reap the harvest of souls. I'm praying you are one of those *unlikely* volunteers, one of the workers Jesus referenced.

---

[16] Mt. 28:18-20, Mark15:15-16, Lk. 24:47, and Acts 1:8.

You might even say, "That couldn't be me. It just isn't likely. I'm not brave enough, smart enough, spiritual enough, rich enough, humble enough, strong enough to be such a worker for Jesus. I am totally unlikely for the job."

Good news (or perhaps scary for you). Jesus was a frequenter, companion, and friend of the socially and religiously *unlikely*. We learn from this text (Jn. 4) and from experts on Jewish customs at the time of Jesus that a rabbi (Jewish teacher) such as Jesus, let alone any Jew, would be unlikely to have a conversation with a Samaritan, especially this Samaritan woman. Samaritans were commonly considered half-breeds, dogs, yes, mongrels by the spiritually, culturally and socially self-superior religious Jews of the day. Considered even worse were women of less than proper reputations (verses 9-17), Samaritan women of ill-repute. Jews of that day were repulsed by Samaritans. In their eyes they were dirty, unclean, and simply undesirable to be around.

The Holy Scriptures are blatantly clear, from Genesis to Revelation, that those who *must* receive care, love, and resources first and foremost from government, society and the Church are the rejected, the outcastes, the marginalized, epitomized by the poor and people affected by disabilities.

The first time I volunteered at a camp for people affected by disabilities, a Joni and Friends Family Retreat in Indiana in 2001, I was provided with an experience that sorely tested my heart attitudes and my spiritual mettle. I had thought of myself as fairly compassionate and giving, especially for those who are marginalized by society, as these folks were one of my focuses as a human being, a Christian, and a pastor.

After receiving orientation and training on ministering to those with disabilities, I contemplated about whom the person might be that I would be caring for during the coming week. As I pondered this matter, a young man came into my room, an older teenager in a wheelchair, being pushed by his younger brother. The teen had obvious intellectual disabilities and was severely spastically challenged. He was nonverbal, except for grunts and groans and a sort of moaning. And HE WAS *DROOLING*! I mean long, stringy, jelly-like drool. (I ask for forbearance from my friends who have such side-affects from their disability. God is using you to confront the pride in the rest of us. We are the unlovely in the eyes of God, those who look down upon others.)

For many people drool is no problem. For me, sadly, drool was an issue. I nearly vomited. I gagged a bit as I thought about wiping away the drool for the next ninety-six hours as his attendant. The sights and smells of the fish canneries I worked in as a youth paled in comparison as far as my drool induced roller coaster stomach was concerned. I was accustomed to decaying, smelly fish guts, but not drool. I was about to discover that this beautiful young man in a wheel chair was God's servant in bringing conviction of sin to my heart. He wasn't the problem. He was not a problem at all. I was.

So, standing there in the same room with this young man and his sibling, I asked myself, "What am I going to do if I have to wipe that line of thick drool over and over again?" As soon as I asked the question I experienced guilt and shame rising in my heart. Then gradually a desire, that was at first motivated by pride (I didn't want to appear to be unspiritual in front of my peers), began to take hold as I collected courage and my faith in Christ.

I pushed forward mentally and emotionally to accept the fact that my week might be preoccupied with this young man and the drool, which was nauseating to me and most probably not to others. As it turned out he wasn't my charge for that week. Nonetheless, God showed me what I was truly made of, or more appropriately, what I wasn't made of. The words of Jack Nicholson in the movie *A Few Good Men* nailed me. "You can't handle the truth!" You're absolutely right, Mr. Nicholson, i.e. Col. Nathan R. Jessep. But I'm working on it.

Disability ministry will ruthlessly test your Christian mettle and your spiritual resolve.

How shameful and disgraceful of me to impose such a view and attitude toward this young man who in and of himself had absolutely done nothing wrong.

I wish I remembered the young man's name so I could repent before him, ask for his forgiveness, and thank him for his ministry to me. Jesus will credit it to his account.

These dear people like this young man are not "them," they are "us."

Friend, you also may be uncomfortable around the *unlikely*, the unlovely, those who are different than typical. Experience would say there is a high probability that you are. That's okay. You don't have to go there alone. Jesus will lead you to minister to those He was preoccupied with—the shut-in and the shut-out, the least, the last, and the lost. In fact, you will meet Jesus there. In Luke 14:13-14, Jesus promises that you will be blessed as you reach out to those affected by disability.

Remember what Jesus said in John 4:34: *My food is to do the will of Him who sent Me, and to finish His work.*

Friends, we also have the will of God to do, and to finish the great work He has given us. There are one-billion-plus people affected by disabilities worldwide, including some fifty-eight million people in the U.S.,[17] waiting to hear and feel the touch of Christ through your voice and your hands. They and their caretakers and loved ones are waiting for you and me.

As you traverse the following chapters, you will gain a greater appreciation for this very specific *work* left to be *finished* by Christ followers. And that means you and me, brothers and sisters in Christ. And you, too, yet to be followers of Christ, come on along with us. You may find it exciting to follow Jesus. You may find Jesus and authentic Christianity to be entirely appealing.

I trust you will be as challenged and blessed as I have become as I continue to discover the delights of God by doing just what Jesus did in hanging out with the *unlikely*, as we, the also *unlikely*, respond to Christ's call and command.

Chapter Three
Nick's Note

Hey, if ever there was a bloke who was most unlikely to become a world evangelist, it was Nick Vujicic—from a working class family in a working class town from the land down under, who was born

[17] U.S. Census Bureau report.

with no arms or legs. I do have my drumstick. You'll have to watch one of my videos to learn about my drumstick.

On the other hand (pun intended), World Evangelists Greg Laurie and Luis Palau are well educated, good looking chaps with all of their legs and arms intact. Not even a drumstick between them!

Starting at age nineteen, God gave me a vision in reaching around the world with the Good News of Jesus.

And in spite of my challenges, perhaps because of them, God has chosen to use me. The dream God gave me is coming true because of His great power and kindness.

No doubt many of you see yourself as unlikely to do anything significant. Perhaps you think of yourself as not smart enough, not tall enough, not good-looking enough, not rich enough, not educated enough...yea, you get the picture.

Americans have a term they use for lies—hogwash. Don't believe that negative hogwash. Jesus said that we could do all things through Him. If you don't believe you can do great things with Jesus's help, then your Jesus isn't big enough.

Have Jesus grow up in you as you become more like him by reading and thinking about His Word, praying for God's dream for you, and the favor he will give you to accomplish great things for him.

Start by just caring for one person who is different; one person who others make fun of or avoid; one person who may be bullied or teased.

Start changing one life at a time with consistent love. You will, in turn, experience divine transformation. Jesus made an incredible statement in Matthew Chapter 25, which boils down to this. *If you serve others you are serving Me.* Wow! And then wow backwards: Wow! When you help someone else Jesus considers it as ministering to Him. That is awesome!

Ministering to one life becomes two and two three and…yea, you again get the picture.

In doing so, Jesus will become bigger in your heart and life.

- Chapter Four -

God's Power in Weakness

As millions of mothers around the world struggled with the daily care for their children with disabilities—wiping soiled and sweated brows, comforting with kisses hands deformed by atrophy, begging for morsels of bread, and sometimes selling their bodies for the same, pulling behind them a child whose limbs no longer respond to his or her brain, weeping with hopelessness in places like Nairobi, Cairo, Krasnodar, Shanghai, Lima, Bangalore and yes even in New York City and Los Angeles—a gathering of people, themselves affected by disabilities, conferred, prayed and planned during a little noticed event in Southeast Asia.

It was called the Forum for World Evangelization 2004, a rather extraordinary conclave of Christian leaders from across the globe gathered in Pattaya, Thailand, to mark the progress and challenges in reaching the world for Christ.

The 2004 Congress produced white papers, which included findings, declarations, and recommendations to the Church universal in this impressive gathering of clergy and lay Christian leaders. One of these white papers[18] declared: "The Savior's words in Luke 14:12-14 provide an irrefutable mandate to the church to reach out to people with disabilities with the gospel: *When you give a dinner or a supper, do not ask your friends, your brothers, your relatives, nor rich neighbors, lest they also invite you back, and you be repaid. But when you give a feast, invite the poor, the maimed, the lame, the blind. And you will be blessed, because they cannot repay you; for you shall be repaid at the resurrection of the just.*"

The clarion and clear call is to reach people affected by disabilities who comprise the most neglected and arguably largest Christ-targeted grouping of people in the world.

The Luke 14:12-24 Mandate, reaching the world's people affected by disability, is not merely an interesting text in the fuller context of Luke, but it is consistent with the *entire focus* of the Gospel of Luke, and is a steady current that flows throughout the biblical record.[19]

Jesus turned the attitudes about disability, brokenness, and weakness on their heads by confronting the religious institutions and leaders of the day, who in their pride had marginalized everyone except those like themselves; not at all unlike political parties and various religious groups today, including some Christian groups. We see this even at the outset of the beginning of the overall context for Luke 14:12-24, the Later Perean Ministry, when

---

[18] Ministry Among People with Disabilities – Lausanne Occasional Paper No. 35 B

[19] *Explore the Book*, J. Sidlow Baxter, Zondervan, 1974, p. 230.

Jesus, on the Sabbath, healed a severely oppressed, elderly lady who had a humiliating disability.

Let's just face up to it. All of us as humans are broken. Apart from Christ we are simply not whole. All our parts are not present. Even as Christ's redeemed people we Christians are still under reconstruction by the Lord Jesus.

Being confronted with such visible object lessons of brokenness, weakness, and vulnerability (people affected by disabilities) causes us to marginalize such people for we are prone to marginalizing our own brokenness and vulnerabilities. Being transparent and authentic is so foreign to our culture. The only remedy for the brokenness of our sin is receiving the Good News of Jesus Christ (Romans 3:23-26) in word and deed. The ensuing redemption (repair work) follows a lifelong commitment to learn of and follow the Master healer and redeemer.

In the second century, Christians along with Jews were some of the most disdained people in the Roman Empire, and thus the most marginalized and persecuted. One of the earliest ways Christians began to get a foothold into the Roman culture, to exist without threat of persecution, and to have an influence on the culture, was to maintain graveyards. What an ignoble beginning. But it was in these humbling conditions that God began, after the death of the Apostles, to bring the Gospel of Jesus Christ to the Gentiles (Romans in this case). Grave keepers! How ironic. God used the lowly occupation of grave keepers to bring the resurrection life of Jesus Christ to the death-bound Roman culture.

What powerful witness in weakness.

Similarly, I contend that God intends, in this generation, to use those affected by disabilities to show forth the power and glory of His name through His broken Church. And yet, as Church leaders and members, many want to impress the world with…well…what the world is impressed with—perfected programs, charismatic speakers, awesome buildings, big budgets, influence, glitzy media presentations, and a shopping mall of programs and services. With these church attributes, we wittingly or unwittingly put on airs, which state that we are not broken at all. None of these attributes of the church is necessarily wrong if done for the right purpose, in humility, and with the right theological and personal motivation. Yet, such attributes are not, I am increasingly convinced, the most compelling characteristics for a skeptical world.

In failing to see God's power in weakness, we miss key components of what Jesus is like and what His Kingdom is supposed to be like. Humility can go a long ways in God's economy for *He gives more grace. Therefore He says: 'God resists the proud, But gives grace to the humble.'* (Jam. 4:6) Hanging out with those affected by disabilities can bring the open heart a maximum dose of humility. People affected by disabilities have a lot to teach us in word and deed. Try it. You'll see for yourself.

Similarly, just as the power of Jesus is discovered in *the weakness of the cross* (1 Cor. 1:18) and in the simple preaching of the Gospel, we will see God means to use people with disabilities as a fundamental component in fulfilling His work on planet earth in a powerful way. We gain insights into this through the international work of Joni and Friends, as government after government, even in those countries that inhibit or prohibit the preaching of the Gospel—such as Cuba and the People's Republic of China, and certain Muslim nations—permit Joni and Friends' emissaries to share the good news of Christ in deed and word. The same is true of Nick Vujicic, a worldwide motivational speaker and evangelist who has no arms or legs.

Joni and Friends comes to give the gift of mobility in Christ's name through its Wheels for the World program, with teams partly made up of people with disabilities and family members affected by those with disabilities. Again, here we have powerful witness in weakness. God turns a symbol of brokenness, a wheelchair, into a platform to boldly proclaim the Gospel, not unlike what He did with a cross, which bore the broken, disabled body of His Son.

The poor and disabled are the prime examples of the type of people God delights in selecting for His purposes. Jesus did so. And so should we.

> *Because the foolishness of God is wiser than men, and the weakness of God is stronger than men. For you see your calling, brethren, that not many wise according to the flesh, not many mighty, not many noble, are called. But God has chosen the foolish things of the world to put to shame the wise, and God has chosen the weak things of the world to put to shame the things which are mighty; and the base things of the world and the things which are despised God has chosen, and the things which are not, to bring to nothing the things that are, that no flesh should glory in His presence.* - I Co. 1:25-29

> *Listen, my dear brothers: Has not God chosen those who are poor in the eyes of the world to be rich in faith and to inherit the kingdom he promised those who love him?* - Jam. 2:5

It appears from these Bible texts that people affected by disabilities and the poor are the chosen people of the New Testament, gifted with faith and destined for God's Kingdom.

Since the scripture says that God delights in manifesting His power in weakness (II Co. 12:9), perhaps we would see a more vibrant, attractive, Spirit-filled Church, founded not upon man's wisdom, but upon the power of God by admitting to and embracing weakness—ours and others. What a relief to people who are interested in Christianity to know they don't have to be perfect to come to Jesus and never will be when on this side of heaven. We, as Christians and the Church, may not say this, but our actions often display this.

Yes, I am convinced we are onto something here.

> *I was with you in weakness,*[20] *in fear, and in much trembling. And my speech and my preaching were not with persuasive words of human wisdom, but in demonstration of the Spirit and of power, that your faith should not be in the wisdom of men but in the power of God.* - I Co. 2:3-5

It is possible that the greatest untapped expeditionary force in the hands of God, one of the greatest instruments in finally ushering in His Kingdom in these tumultuous and troubling times, is this *unlikely* grouping of people and those who radically love them and serve them in embracing their weakness and ours. Yes, this is crazy, totally upside down to normal thinking, but not in the economy of God's Kingdom.

Come. Join with the army of the last to be considered and the least suspecting. Typical able-bodied men, women, youth and children—yet weak—are welcome to volunteer.

---

[20] "Asthenia" in the Greek, i.e. feebleness physically

Chapter Four
Nick's Note

Power in weakness. My friend Dan'l has really got it going here.

Your lack is God's opportunity to fill in the blanks and do something big in you and through you.

I count it a privilege to be a friend of Joni Eareckson Tada. She is one awesome Christian lady.

Think about this. God knew exactly what He was doing when He allowed her, at seventeen years of age, to end a promising athletic, academic, and professional career by diving into the Chesapeake Bay, snapping her neck, and leaving her paralyzed from the neck down.

From a then depressed, broken girl, a patient in a Stryker bed in a dark rehabilitation center, God through His Word slowly built a new woman. This woman God would eventually use to birth and grow an international Christ-honoring ministry, which is making a major impact as a leader in fostering a worldwide disability ministry movement.

Jesus has picked all kinds of imperfect people throughout history and around the world today to perform mighty feats for His namesake.

See yourself as one of them.

- Chapter Five -

The Ministry of Incarnation and Touch

In the later months of 1995, when I was about a year into the midnight of my soul, I desperately missed the touch of Christ's presence. I also yearned to be touched by another human. My home had pulsated for many years with the lives of my daughters, my wife, and scores of kids from our church youth group, as well as a Tuesday evening Bible fellowship with new believers.

I was accustomed to lots of human interaction with hugs, laughter, and all the blessings that close friendships and warm fellowship bring to a home. As my marriage was clearly ending so was my pastoral ministry life. After resigning from my church, my home became desolate, except for my pal Jake, my Labrador Retriever. Then Jake's arthritis became crippling and he had to be put down. I wept as I left the veterinary clinic. My house was transformed into a human "hugless" and "touchless" wasteland. Loneliness became my constant companion.

I learned the hard way that loneliness is a continual ache.

I longed for human touch, and I don't mean in a sexual way, albeit that was missed as well. Following the loss of my marriage, I remember a time when a woman friend simply touched my hand. The tangible emotional and physical high I experienced was startling. As humans we are wired to touch and be touched. God understands this on a personal basis as the Gospel of Luke reveals.

The most chronic and consistent form of suffering reported by people affected by disability is surprisingly not physical pain, but rather it is loneliness and thus, the need to be touched, to be embraced, to be included.

Luke's Gospel and the larger context of this book—Luke 14:12-24—is about God through Christ compassionately touching humanity.

When I walked away from Christianity as a young man, my parting prayer to God was "God, if you are real and reveal yourself to me, I will serve you for the rest of my life. But I don't want any religious phony baloney." Yep, I actually prayed those exact words. So when God, much to my amazement, revealed Himself to me in a travel trailer in Vancouver, Washington, on a cold September night in 1970, my life was tangibly touched by the reality of God—a mega compassion connection.

At our core that's what every human was made to know—to experience the tangible life-changing presence of God in Christ. Generally speaking, people apart from Christ do not know what it is they long for. They are lonely for the touch only God can bring to their hearts and their life experiences.

We are made to know God and know him experientially. Devoid of this there is an absence, a shadow of loneliness even in a crowded room; for some even an ache, a sense of not being connected, fulfilled or completed. A point of view where many in their secret fears sense they face the world alone, even with loved ones about. We can be fairly effective at pushing that down and out through stuff and activities, but it always remains with us at some level if we are not connected to God.

Many Christians, perhaps too many, have been too long without the touch of God.

Following creation, without question the greatest act of God involving humanity was the incarnation of Jesus. God *became flesh and dwelt among us.* [21] God came and touched humanity. He became one of us. He ate and discoursed with us. He walked with us. He laughed with us. He suffered with us. He wept with us. He suffered for us. It's not that He couldn't relate to us. Rather we couldn't relate well to Him. So onto the stage of time and place came Jesus, the Son of the Living God.

As the Apostle John noted, [22] *The one who existed from the beginning is the one we have heard and seen. We saw him with our own eyes and touched him with our own hands. He is Jesus Christ, the word of life.* (NLT)

I think these men who surrounded Jesus were huggers. Hugging and cheek kissing guys are very Middle Eastern, as was, I suspect, the man Christ Jesus.

---

[21] Jn. 1:14, I Tim. 3:16, Col. 1:15.

[22] 1 Jn. 1:1, NLT.

Jesus not only became human, the ultimate God-man, but he touched humanity, up close and personally. This was one of the signatures of Christ's life and ministry—especially noted for touching the untouched and the untouchable.

God knows that the human race desperately needs His touch, every person one at a time. He has done something about it. And He continues to do something about it. This is the genesis of the Christian saying, "I'm lost without you." And with this condition clearly in his mind our famous physician Luke writes his great biography of Jesus. Jesus longs for us, too: *O Jerusalem, Jerusalem…how often I have longed to gather your children together, as a hen gathers her chicks under her wings, but you were not willing!* [23] The Parable of the Prodigal Son [24] is about God longing for fellowship with us in spite of our sin and rebellion.

This may be hard for you to get your brain and heart around, but let me say, "God is madly in love with you." See the passion of the Cross so we might bridge our sin, our daily sin, to His acceptance and presence every day. The Cross is His Great Embrace, the ultimate compassion connector.

So it's not surprising that this Gospel of Luke and The Lost Mandate are all about us and God's tangible, up-front, close love for us.

The Gospel of Luke, among its unique qualities, is distinctive from the other three Gospels with its clear emphasis upon Jesus as the Son of Man, the humanity of Christ.

---

[23] Lk. 13:34, NIV.

[24] Lk. 15:11-31.

The Gospel according to Luke "has a *very human beginning*… Right away we are in the hearts and homes and hopes of simple-living, godly, likeable folk—Zacharias and Elisabeth, Joseph and Mary, 'neighbors and cousins,' shepherds, Simeon, Anna… As we press on into the succeeding chapters, we soon begin to sense that this marked attention to the *human* is not only our first clue but the *main key.*"[25] (underline emphasis mine)

This focus on Christ's humanity and on humankind in general, regular folks like many of you and me, continues as a powerful eddy throughout the current of this Gospel, affecting the flow of the grand literary sea of all four Gospels.

In the twenty major parables within the Gospel of Luke, all but two begin with *"There was a certain man..."* (italics mine)

His touch is everywhere throughout the Gospels:

- *So He touched her hand, and the fever left her. And she arose and served them. - Mtt. 8:15*
- *Then He touched their eyes, saying, "According to your faith let it be to you." - Mtt. 9:29*
- *So Jesus had compassion and touched their eyes. And immediately their eyes received sight, and they followed Him. - Mtt. 20:34*
- *Then Jesus, moved with compassion, stretched out His hand and touched him, and said to him, "I am willing; be cleansed." - Mk. 1:41*
- *And He took him aside from the multitude, and put His fingers in his ears, and He spat and touched his tongue. - Mk. 7:33*
- *And He took them in His arms and began blessing them, laying His hand on them. - Mk.10:16*

---

[25] Ibid., p. 243.

- *Then He put out His hand and touched him, saying, "I am willing; be cleansed." Immediately the leprosy left him.* - *Lk. 5:13*
- *And they were bringing even their babies so that He would touch them...* - *Lk. 18:15*
- *But Jesus answered and said, "Permit even this. And He touched his ear and healed him."* - *Lk. 22:51*

He was and is the King of Contagious Love and compassion connectors.

This was all very much in keeping with the style of Jesus's ministry—personal, up-front, close, and physical—extending His loving heart through His loving hands.

I'm drawn to Jesus's ministry to children. It provides another intimate look at the ministry of touch our Master practiced. In Mark 10:15-16 we read of Jesus *Then He took the children into His arms and placed His hands on their heads and blessed them.* (NLT) The original Greek text expands our understanding as this was more than the perfunctory touching of a person's forehead, which one might see at an ecclesiastical function. Jesus took the children *into His arms, placed His hands on their heads,* and *blessed them.* He spent personal, intimate, loving time with them, one at a time—embracing them physically and speaking words of blessing intimately to them. He was no different with people affected by disabilities.

He personally experienced and thus understood loneliness [26] and our need for affirmation by close physical proximity and touch. We, as Christians, should aspire to be nothing less than our Master.

---

[26] Mk. 15:34; Mt. 26:40.

One of my special blessings has been to serve on the Board of Directors of, and then be employed by, a worldwide ministry called Life Without Limbs, founded by world evangelist, Nick Vujicic. Nick is a phenomenon to the world and Christendom. Nick's ministry signature is 'hugs.' Nick touches the world with the life giving message of Christ, driven home by his desire to hug with his neck everyone he meets. In doing so he represents the Lord he serves.

Similarly, I was pleasantly surprised and impressed with Pope Benedict. When my wife, Colette, and I were on vacation in Italy we were unexpectedly provided passes to attend Benedict's second papal audience. We ended up sitting just a few yards from his dais as he preached in St. Peter's Square. As Pope Benedict stepped off the Popemobile to the immediate left of his podium sat scores of religious and secular dignitaries, and on his right were approximately thirty people in wheelchairs. Before addressing the dignitaries or the throng in the square, he personally took time to individually touch and pray for each person sitting in a wheel chair. Wow! What a statement to the crowd about the economy of God's kingdom, where the least and last are the greatest, most honored guests.

I repeat, the most common suffering expressed by people with disabilities is surprisingly not pain, but…loneliness, which of course has its unique form of accompanying emotional and psychological pain. People affected by disabilities can be in a crowd of thousands or in the midst of just a handful of people, yet due to their circumstances become isolated and lonely. The most common need is simple recognition, just to be a part without undue attention and to be touched with friendship and laughter.

So be a great compassion connector for God. You may be the only Jesus people see and the only Jesus from whom they receive a touch.

Chapter Five
Nick's Note

Anyone who knows me, sees me at gatherings, or watches me on video or on television knows I love human touch. God has totally put that in our human software. At the end of every message at every venue, I spend time afterwards hugging as many people as possible, literally hundreds at a time…at times thousands.

It was the year I started my ministry, when I was nineteen, when a girl came up crying and hugged me, telling me that no one had ever told her that they loved her. From that day on, God gave me a love for people to reach them with His love. From that day on, I began hugging everyone I could with the love of Jesus. From that day on, I began telling everyone I love them. From that day on, I began telling everyone and anyone that God loves them. Because it's true!

Dan'l told me one day that the signature of my ministry is hugs. In fact I do hold the Guinness World Record for the most hugs in an hour—1749. In my young life I may have hugged more people than anyone on the face of the earth.

I know for certain that so far I have given over 360,000 hugs.

I hug because……………well, wholesome healthy human touch is powerful. It's healing.

I know that wholesome, healthy hugs reach the soul.

The fact is we need a daily touch from God…a daily hug from God. His spiritual hugs keep me going with zest and zeal. Can't live without them.

God asks us as His people, since he doesn't physically hug us, to make sure that we hug each other for Jesus. The Bible says we followers of Jesus are the 'body of Christ,' therefore we are his hands and feet.

It makes me think of what the Apostle John said in his first letter verse 19: "We love Him because he first loved us." Through my life I can say, "I hug Him because He first hugged me." John adds to this (vs. 11) "Beloved, if God so love us, we also ought to love one another." So let's be hugged by God and lovingly and wholesomely hug others.

This makes me think of Garry Phelps, a twenty-five-year-old guy with Downs Syndrome, who is a hugger. One day he was overhearing a conversation between adults who were saying, "Did you just hear that (so in so) had a daughter who was diagnosed with Downs Syndrome?"

Garry broke out in response to say, "Oh, that's great!"

They looked at him and asked, "What do you mean, Garry? What's so great about having Downs Syndrome?"

Garry responded, "You just love everybody, and you never, ever hurt anybody."

As far as quality, Garry may be the best hugger ever.

- Chapter Six -

Joining God as the Life of the Party

Once a hippie (and having been an all-around clown and party animal in high school) I know a few things about parties…especially parties of the wrong kind. Not just a few people might be surprised to learn that God loves parties...parties of the right kind. Jesus, in our primary text in Luke 14, speaks about partying with the least, the last, the shut-in and the shutout.

> *12 Then he also said to him who invited him, "When you give a dinner or a supper, do not ask your friends, your brothers, your relatives, nor rich neighbors, lest they also invite you back, and you be repaid. 13 But when you give a feast, invite the poor, the maimed, the lame, the blind. 14 And you will be blessed, because they cannot repay you; for you shall be repaid at the resurrection of the just.*

> *…Then He said to him, "A certain man gave a great supper and invited many, 17 and sent his servant at supper time to say to those who were invited, 'Come, for all things are now ready.' 18 But they*

all with one accord began to make excuses. The first said to him, 'I have bought a piece of ground, and I must go and see it. I ask you to have me excused.' 19 And another said, 'I have bought five yoke of oxen, and I am going to test them. I ask you to have me excused.' 20 Still another said, 'I have married a wife, and therefore I cannot come.' 21 So that servant came and reported these things to his master. Then the master of the house, being angry, said to his servant, 'Go out quickly into the streets and lanes of the city, and bring in here the poor and the maimed and the lame and the blind.' 22 And the servant said, 'Master, it is done as you commanded, and still there is room' 23 Then the master said to the servant, 'Go out into the highways and hedges, and compel them to come in, that my house may be filled. 24 For I say to you that none of those men who were invited shall taste my supper.'

The Bible, from cover to cover, is replete with references to feasts, banquets, and celebrations. In fact, most feasts recorded in Holy Scripture were ordered by God for His people to celebrate. How about that! Ordered to celebrate, ordered to have parties!

God is the eternal banquet host Jesus is referring to in Luke 14, who has called His people to celebrate with him the life we have as the family of God. It's difficult to imagine a happier command to follow than being ordered to have a feast with God and with a group of loving celebratory people!

Jesus revealed His passion for fellowship when at His last supper he instituted communion with the twelve disciples. He declared, ...*With fervent desire I have desired to eat this Passover with* you... (Lk. 22:15) Throughout the Gospels we get the picture that he liked hanging out with people in feasting and celebration, such being the case in the feasts at the homes of the tax collectors Matthew and Zaccheus. [27]

The prophet, Isaiah, wrote of the end-of-time great banquet, which I believe, and a good number of scholars will agree, is the fulfillment of the same banquet that Jesus speaks about in Luke 14:

> *On this mountain the Lord Almighty will prepare a feast of rich food for all peoples, a banquet of aged wine—the best of meats and the finest of wines. On this mountain He will destroy the shroud that enfolds all peoples, the sheet that covers all nations; He will swallow up death forever. The Sovereign Lord will wipe away the tears from all faces; He will remove the disgrace of his people from all the earth. The Lord has spoken.* (Is. 25:6-8, NIV)

Jesus began the miraculous aspect of His public ministry by making sure a wedding party was all it should be for His mother's Jewish friends. (Jn. 2:1-11) The wedding feast at Cana was about to be a failure, but God made sure that a wedding in a little country town was not going to be joyless and did so through the miracle working power of His Son. Imagine the chatter this must have precipitated amongst the host and guests. Mary had to be so much more than a pleased and proud mama. Jesus no doubt was blessed to be able to meet the needs of His mother and her friends. Any loving son would feel that way.

Here, in Luke 14:23, we see that God commands us to reach marginalized people for Him so that His "house will be full." In the original language "full" means bursting at the seams. So it's not just

---

[27] Mtt. 9:10, Lk. 19:5.

a very fine party; it is a *huge* celebration with an unprecedented crowd. And not only is it huge, it is forever.

So the banquet Luke 14 speaks about will never find its equal on this side of heaven. However, we can get a taste of heaven, of God's Kingdom, as we bring the poor and those affected by disability into the life of God's house by going out and compelling them to come into the Church and then celebrating Christ with them. (Lk. 14:23)

In fact, some churches literally obey this text and host Luke 14 Banquets—inviting the poor and people affected by disabilities into the Church where they serve them, honor them and provide a first rate feast for all. Such is the case at what is called the 'Big Pink Church of Charlotte,' Calvary Church in Charlotte, NC. It's an incredible celebration, yet a mere foretaste of what is to come and a mere shadow of what should be going on in the daily life of the Church.

I urge you to experience Christ in the face of the poor and in the pain of the afflicted. It is often a party. He will surprise you with His joyful presence when you minister for and to Him in these places of suffering.

Henry Blackaby in his now famous book *Experiencing God* [28] brings out a powerful ministry principle, which essentially says, "Figure out where God is working and join him there." Friends, God has flashing green arrows with reverberating sound effects pointing to the poor and the people affected by disabilities. Join God and

---

[28] *Experiencing God*, Henry Blackaby, LifeWay Press, Nashville, TN. Year?

experience God as never before in the face of the poor and in the presence of those affected by disabilities.

Endless fields of souls are ready to meet the Savior—myriads upon myriads wait with receptive hearts to hear the gospel and to experience the light shining in their dark places. They are waiting to become your brothers and sisters in Christ. And when they do, there is a party in heaven.[29]

Never forget that the word 'evangelize' in the New Testament literally means 'to tell good tidings.' We bring life changing, foot stomp'n, hallelujah high five'n, buckets full of good news. We report on what Jesus has done for others, what he has done for us, and what he will do for them. And then He does it. To those who will let Him in, He transforms. He uplifts. He enables. He empowers. He parties with them.

In summary then, here in Luke 14 we have Jesus attending a feast put on by a prominent Pharisee. (vs. 1) In the Parable of the Great Banquet (vs.15-24) God the Father invites all, but especially the poor and those affected by disabilities (vs. 13, 21, 23) to His feast. He tells His servants that He is *angry* that His banquet house is not filled with such people and urges them with passion to *go out quickly* and to *compel them* (literally, make them come in, or hook them by the arm and pull them along) to come *into my house.*

It is evident from this parable that those who were well-to-do were not inclined to answer God's invitation. However, those in need were more disposed to do so. People in need, who are often painfully aware of their own needs, have a greater appreciation for

[29] Luke 15:7

what God has to offer. Again, that's why James calls the poor, "heirs to the Kingdom." (2:5) They are ready and waiting to receive the good news. People who have a desperate need for the Good News, who are poor in spirit, have an advantage in seeing their desperate need for God. *Blessed are the poor in spirit for theirs is the Kingdom of God.* [30]

God the Father makes it very clear that the ultimate feast at the end of time and Christian fellowship in this life will not be what it should be unless the poor and people affected by disabilities have their full representation at His table. It's up to us to see that they are present—now!

Come. Join us in this great proclamation of the Good News, inviting the poor and people affected by disabilities to enter the banquet hall to meet the great host of heaven, so that we all will indeed be blessed.

Party on!

Chapter Six
Nick's Note

Dan'l has told me how he loves to have lunch or dinner with my Serbian relatives and friends. Serbians are all about family. We always look forward to our dinners, banquets, and parties. I love celebration experiences when I am with Christians worshipping the Lord, whether at home, in a church building, a restaurant, or a mountain top.

---

[30] Mtt. 5:30, NIV.

I was a bit captivated by the story about the Scottish Monk, Angus, experiencing closeness with God when up in a high mountain meadow in Scotland. I can totally relate to him describing being close to God as the 'thin places.' That is, when heaven and earth, when the divine and us come in contact with each other. It's a compassion connection.

I anticipate with expectancy, and count myself honored for those special times when I am really near with the Lord, sensing him breathing and speaking into my heart and life. Sometimes it's when I fast and pray for a season. Other times it's when I am speaking, and I know the power of God is emanating from me to others, watching God the Holy Spirit transform lives. Sometimes I am just going about my day when I sense him close. That's just awesome. And like Angus, sometimes it is in the splendor of nature that I experience closeness with God.

I hope you have special parties, celebrations with God and God's family. He desires to be close, very close with you.

The Bible tells us if you will "Come near to God…he will come near to you." (Jam. 4:8a - GNT)

- Chapter Seven -

It Begins with a Lady

Luke 13:10-17

Just before crossing the Jordan into what is called the Later Perean Ministry, the scene begins at a Sabbath synagogue service when Christ comes across an oppressed, older woman who the scripture says had been *crippled by a spirit. She was bent over and could not straighten up at all.* (Lk. 13:10-11, NIV) This description calls to my memory images of Mother Theresa in her later years.

While Mother Theresa was diminutive and stooped over, this unfortunate lady in Luke 13 was in a much worse condition. She was afflicted by a demonic spirit that caused *astheneias (Greek text)* or a *lack of strength,* and was *en sunkuptousa* or *bowed together.* Thus her back was probably parallel to the ground, if not bent over more. This was an extreme case of curvature of the spine.

So the story of the Luke 14 Mandate begins with this devout Jewish lady who came to worship the one and only true God in a synagogue, probably as she had faithfully done so Saturday after Saturday for many years. Perhaps she heard that the prophet, rumored to be a man destined for kingship, would be present at the synagogue. She might have been wondering if somehow this reported miracle worker would make a spiritual, even a physical difference in her life. Or perhaps she faithfully went to Sabbath worship, and Jesus of Galilee just 'happened' to be at her place of worship.

However it occurred in her mind, God in His sovereignty chose this broken, bent-over, oppressed lady to begin something of historic proportion—a disability ministry movement, which would emerge on the Church and world scene some 2,000 years later.

Once again we watch Christ choosing to focus His attention on the unlikely. *He was teaching.* The Greek, *en didaskon,* is in the periphrastic imperfect active, which implies that *as* Jesus was speaking He became aware of this woman. *And behold (Kai idou) or And look* lets us know He suddenly became aware of her and *called her to him.* The Master, seeing those in need and suffering, calls them to Himself. Those who see their need respond to the call.

First Jesus declares that this woman is free, and then lays His hands on her to impart healing. So tender is he, our beloved Savior doesn't merely speak her healing and dismiss her. Rather, he compassionately touches her, putting His loving hands upon her as if to say, "I care for you with a genuine love, beloved worshipper of the one and true God."

No doubt aware of the years of ridicule and mean spirited words she had endured, He speaks words of respect, *Woman, you are made whole.* Unlike today, when calling a female *woman* is usually demeaning, in Jesus's culture, use of the word woman was an act of respect, honoring such a lady.

> *And immediately she was made straight, and glorified God.* (vs. 13)

The next word in the following verse (14) of this compelling narrative is small yet powerful in its implication, and that word is *but.*

> *But the ruler of the synagogue answered with indignation, because Jesus had healed on the Sabbath…*

When Jesus saw this woman and called her out, He was well aware that controversy was brewing once again. Christ understood that healing on the Sabbath, especially in a synagogue, would reignite the hot coals of conflict between the religious rulers and Himself. It appears some had trailed Him from Jerusalem into Perea to stir up even more opposition, and to find more reasons to condemn Him.

On three previous occasions He had been called 'the devil' or was accused of working on behalf of the devil as He went about teaching and healing.[31]

The religious, haughty spirits of today continue such opposition to the work of Christ.

Let's reengage with the narrative as another blunt rebuke is about to come.

---

[31] Mk. 3:22, Mt. 9:27-34, Lk. 11:14-36

> *But the ruler of the synagogue answered with indignation, because Jesus had healed on the Sabbath; and He said to the crowd, "There are six days on which men ought to work; therefore come and be healed on them, and not on the Sabbath day."* (13:14)

Answered with indignation. The Greek word *aganakte* for indignation comes from a base word from which we get the English transliteration 'to agonize.' This religious leader reacted with a pained response that brought with it scorn. It was a type of self-righteous "who-do-you-think-you-are?" indignation. How dare Jesus heal in the house of God on the Sabbath day! This ruler of the synagogue was truly and painfully upset. True to even hypocrites, legalists, and those indifferent in the church today, this ruler had genuine feelings and reactions, but they certainly were from wrong-headed thinking and theology, not least of which was a callousness of heart.

It was a religious spirit at play. Not unlike certain militant fundamentalist Islamic clergy who spew hatred and destruction of others—especially Christians and Jews. And then there are the militant Islamic counterparts, who spew their own hatred such as the Westboro Baptist Church, in [32] Topeka, Kansas. The WBC's clergy and followers are verbally vicious towards gays and lesbians, and picket funerals of American servicemen and desecrate the American flag.

Because Jesus had healed on the Sabbath. (ESV) The religious leader's angry reaction was because of Jesus and was directed toward Him.

---

[32] The WBC is not affiliated with any known Baptist conventions or associations and the two largest Baptist denominations, the Baptist World Alliance and the Southern Baptist Convention have denounced the WBC over the years. See http://en.wikipedia.org/wiki/Westboro_Baptist_Church.

But the ruler's following words, according to the Greek grammatical structure were directed at the congregants: *There are six days in which work ought to be done. Come on those days and be healed, and not on the Sabbath day.* (ESV) He was letting the people know "Hey, I'm boss man here. I'm in charge. Stay with the party line. You do what I say. Don't copy what Jesus is doing, nor admire or applaud it. Forget compassion and follow me in being religiously right."

Come on those days and be healed. The duplicity here is rich. The ruler of the synagogue, of course, really had no expectation that this oppressed woman, or anyone else for that matter, would be healed on any other day of the week. The scripture says, *Out of the abundance of the heart the mouth speaks.* (Lk. 6:45) As this hypocrite continued to speak, his true heart was revealed (vs. 17) to his own congregants as he was confronted by Christ.

Hypocrite! Such is Christ's swift and pointed response; a charge directed straight at this man's heart and character, who Christ notes will assist an ox or donkey on the Sabbath, yet does not have even an ounce of care and compassion for this suffering woman.

> *So ought not this woman…be loosed from this bond on the Sabbath?*

So if you are willing to water your donkey on the Sabbath, should you not assist this woman, this broken and suffering woman? This woman, who for eighteen years has born an incredible burden while being a faithful attendee of your synagogue. Should she not be freed from her oppression this very Sabbath day?

> *And when He said these things, all His adversaries were put to shame; and all the multitude rejoiced for all the glorious things that were done by Him.* – Lk. 13:17

The God-man behind enemy lines routs the enemy again!

Put to shame. The NIV reads: *They were humiliated.* They were ashamed, as they should have been.

Chapter Seven
Nick's Note

It's easy to get angry, even disgusted, at the hypocrites who persisted in their brutal verbal assaults upon Jesus. But what really bothers me is the hypocrite in this story who had a total disregard for that little bent over lady. He was more interested in maintaining his position of power and his religious rules and regulations than rejoicing that this woman, who had experienced so much suffering, and was now healed and whole.

The hypocritical religious ruler could have cared less about her. She was just in his way. He was annoyed with her and what Christ had so compassionately done—brought her erect into the dignity of full womanhood.

I suppose many of us have felt little inside, at least at one time or another, perhaps even bent or broken. So we can identify with some of the pain this little lady must have experienced.

As a young lad I was bullied, ignored, made fun of, and even verbally harassed. It could have broken me and bent me over emotionally and spiritually. Yet, while God may have given me a shortened version of the typical body, he has enlarged my heart and empowered my spirit.

A prophet of ancient Israel exhorted us God-followers to "stretch out our tent pegs" so we could make our tent larger and God could fill our larger tent with more of Himself.

A secret I learned when a wee bit of a boy was to begin to trust God for little things, and then larger things, and then great and awesome things. I was stretching my tent pegs. I was putting my faith into action.

Now mate, go stretch your tent pegs.

- Chapter Eight -

The Mustard Seed and the Leaven

> *Then He said, "What is the Kingdom of God like? And to what shall I compare it? It is like a mustard seed, which a man took and put in his garden; and it grew and became a large tree, and the birds of the air nested in its branches."* - Lk. 13:18-19

I remember when my dad, "Ernie" Ernest Markham, would begin the annual planting of vegetables in our backyard. Like his father and grandfather, Daniel and Dan Markham, my dad was compelled to break out his spade every spring, and row by row began to turn the hardened sod. Dad worked the earth over again and again with shovel, then rake, and then by hand, until it was near powder-like.

Next was the task of parsing out all the small pieces of grass, weeds and other unwanted particles. Ah, yes, a good job for his son. I didn't really mind, even though from time to time I wanted to get out of doing this tedious part of gardening. Still, even at a young age I sensed there was something reassuring about working in the soil, especially with my dad, just as previous generations of Markhams had done.

I vividly recall secretly admiring my dad's calloused, tan, weathered, muscular hands with their protruding vessels and veins, especially so as he used the wooden planting plug to push holes into the softened soil. I wanted masculine hands just like Dad.

I would walk behind him, dropping tiny seeds into the dimples of earthen wombs. It was always a marvel to think that from these miniscule kernels would sprout flourishing life, capable of growing into voluminous life-giving plants. Jesus, too, even though He is the creator of all, as man he was obviously captivated by the spectacle of nature and life bearing seeds.

While it is unknown what variety of mustard seed Jesus was speaking about in our text, it could very well have been *Brassica hirta,* a mild white mustard common to North Africa, the Mediterranean and the Middle East.

These smallest of seeds, within a short few months, grow into a tall herb of ten to twelve feet in height, looming over grain crops and vineyards. The mustard seed is as small as one of the letters in this sentence you are reading, yet it has the potential to take a place of major prominence in God's garden, God's Kingdom, and thus the world.

Context is illuminative. It is valuable to recall that this parable is in the immediate context of the story of a diminutive, seemingly unimportant, rejected, woman with a severe disability. This mustard seed of a human being healed, and yes, loved by the Master. (vs. 10-17) Yet, what a huge impact her healing has had, not the least of which was to be used by God to further anger the religious hierarchy, which ended up setting the stage for Christ's arrest and crucifixion, and thus becoming the Savior of the world.

Secondarily, she becomes the gateway to bring about what we see in the larger context of the book of Luke. (especially 13:10 - 17:10) That is, a mandate (14:12-24) yet beginning to be fulfilled today in reaching today's one billion people worldwide who are affected by disabilities.

I think this dear lady would say because of what Jesus did, and continues to do through her suffering, that her suffering was well worth the fruit it has produced and will yet produce.

Again, take notice of the fact that Jesus always paid attention to the little ones, the forgotten ones of the world, the marginalized, the apparently unimportant, the shut-in and the shut-out, the unseen. *What is the kingdom like?* What can it be compared to? Answer: A diminutive, seemingly insignificant lady with a disability whose life is changed by the life giver, who in turn is used by Jesus to spark a discourse about what is to eventually become a worldwide disability ministry movement.

These little seeds remind us of the incredible potential yet to be realized in the Church of Jesus Christ as people with disabilities are fully integrated into the life of the body of Christ. No Bible passage elaborates better on the integration of people with disabilities into the local church than I Corinthians 12:12-27.

The theme of I Corinthians 12 is proper care for the body of Christ (the church) by its individual members and proper care of the individuals by the church. Observe verse 25, which is the reason for this Chapter 12 dissertation by the Apostle Paul:

> *12 The body is a unit, though it is made up of many parts; and though all its parts are many, they form one body. So it is with Christ. 13 For we were all baptized by one Spirit into one body—whether Jews or Greeks, slave or free—and we were all given the one Spirit to drink…20 As it is, there are many parts, but one body. 21 The eye cannot say to the hand, "I don't need you!" And the head cannot say to the feet, "I don't need you!" 22 On the contrary, those parts of the body that seem to be weaker are indispensable, 23 and the parts that we think are less honorable we treat with special honor. And the parts that are unpresentable are treated with special modesty, 24 while our presentable parts need no special treatment. But God has combined the members of the body and has given greater honor to the parts that lacked it, 25 so that there should be no division in the body, but that its parts should have equal concern for each other.* (NIV, underline emphasis mine)

The text reveals that the way to prevent division in the church is to have a culture of 'honoring' one another—each and every one in the body of Christ. In fact, according to this Corinthian text, those who are to be most honored should be the weakest and the most vulnerable. We would be hard pressed to get more counterculture, more prophetic than this.

Look at verse 21 of I Corinthians 12: *I don't need you.* By our actions and inactions, prejudices, secret thoughts, attitudes, and inclusions or exclusions of others, we all, in some measure, say to some members of the body of Christ, "I don't need you." Black, Caucasian, Latino, Asian, Fundamentalist, Evangelical, Reformed, Pentecostal, Catholic, liberal, poor, rich, powerful, obscure, strong, weak, lovely or unlovely—members of Christ's body can be found saying in word or action, "I don't need you."

Verse 22 states, *On the contrary,* that is, *I don't need you* is all wrong; it is fundamentally flawed. Now listen very carefully and closely to what God the Holy Spirit says next: *Those parts of the body that seem to be weaker are indispensable.*

Of all the members of the body, the only ones that this text declares are *indispensable* are those who *seem to be weaker.* The Greek word used for *seem* means 'only appears to be, but not really so' as in an illusion. While we often hear that perception is reality because what people see is real to them, this is not so with theological or philosophical truth. Thus, perceptions can be, and frequently are, false views and just wrong-headed ideas. As Christians, our minds and hearts, and thus perceptions, must align with God's word.

While people with disabilities *seem to be weaker,* in actuality they are *indispensable.* We can't do without them. I have visited and worshipped in scores, perhaps hundreds of churches, of all sizes in various denominations and non-denominations. Most have been Christ-honoring, loving, and Bible centered. But no matter how vibrant and healthy they may be, if they are not inclusive of people with disabilities, they are not all God has designed them to be or wants them to be. In fact, while their buildings may be full of people and programs, they are not yet full or complete as a spiritual body. (Lk. 14:23b)

The word *weaker* (the King James Version translation is *feeble*) literally means strength-less, impotent, without strength, feeble, infirm, sickly, afflicted, distressed, or oppressed. While the New

Testament refers to a variety of disabilities, such as being blind and lame, in I Corinthians 12 we come to an all-encompassing generic word for a wide variety of disabling conditions, a word that could be translated as 'disability.' Thus the verse could read, "Those members that seem to be affected by a disability…"

They appear to be weaker, but most people affected by a disability, who know Christ and those who don't, will tell you their disability has made them stronger. People who know them well will say the same. It is true of all of us in varying degrees—our trials make us stronger. We know that, but often fail to recognize it in people who are frail physically or mentally, or of lower economic or social status. I consider some of the people with disabilities that I know to be the strongest in faith, and the most powerful in mental determination and emotional perseverance. What they have gone through would crush other people. This is why this book is dedicated to Rick Eastin, a minister of the Gospel in Fresno, CA, who happens to be significantly affected by cerebral palsy—a man of great faith and perseverance.

What this text, in part, is saying is that we can survive as the *body* of Christ without certain members—perhaps the nose, an eye, the mouth or an ear—but we must have the pancreas, liver, kidneys, and even that little pituitary gland to have a full life. If we were to look at these internal organs we would say we must have them to be alive at all.

To the human eye the liver is unattractive, unseemly, and so is the heart. This may be, but they only seem to be unattractive. The wonder and beauty of life could not continue if the vital organs such as the heart, liver, or pancreas were absent or didn't function as designed.

The 'apparently' weaker, or the people affected by disabilities, are indispensable just like the pancreas. They are the members that are essential and necessary to our well-being. We can do without a nose, without teeth, without an ear or beautiful cheekbones. However, without the heart or liver or pancreas the whole body fails. In many ways, too much of the Christian culture has been all too affected by this wrong headedness. For too many it is stunning looks, a great body, physical strength, and charisma that are essentials that matter far too much.

Those tiny mustard seeds have a purpose in God's garden and vineyard, the Church. Like mustard, they help to keep disease away, provide nutrition, and offer healing powers, all the while giving flavor, that is appeal, to the body of Christ.

And Then There is the 'Leaven'

God's kingdom is not only like a mustard seed, but also like leaven.

> *And again He said, "To what shall I liken the Kingdom of God? It is like leaven, which a woman took and hid in three measures of meal till it was all leavened."* - Lk. 13:20-21

We had a weekly housewarming ritual at my house when I was a young boy. Often on Thursday night, my dad, a US Navy Seabee World War II veteran, would begin to soak a pot of Navy beans for our regular Saturday noon dinner of Navy bean soup complimented by mom's hot homemade bread and cinnamon rolls. Friday night Dad would cut up bacon and place it—along with some ham hocks and spices, celery, onions, and whatever else might be handy—into the simmering pot of beans.

That same night Mom would mix flour, water, a little salt, oil, milk, and yeast (leaven) in an extra-large yellow bowl. She would knead the bread dough over and over again and then finally let it sit with a white linen towel over the top of the yeast-empowered growing mound of nourishment. Every now and then I was allowed to punch the mound with my fist to deflate it. As a young lad, it was a mystery to me how that mound grew after each punching episode. Unseen to the natural eye, the leaven was invading every portion of the dough, causing it to grow, and grow again, unbeknownst to everyone (at least I thought so) except Mom and me.

Saturday at noon there would be freshly baked bread and cinnamon rolls with hot Navy bean soup. Kids from the neighborhood always showed up. It was a feast of warmth and wholesome goodness. Leaven can do a lot of good.

Like leaven, which is comprised of microorganisms, so it is with people with disabilities, who, while unnoticed under the white linen towel of the world and much of the Church, God is preparing through power of the Holy Spirit to reach the entire mound of the world. Not one portion of the bread is left unaffected by the yeast.

Similarly, people with disabilities know no racial, ethnic, political, geographic, gender, or social boundaries. They are everywhere; usually hidden and out of sight perhaps, but everywhere. Like leaven, they are loaded with the 'mustard seed' potential for the power of God to unleash in all places and peoples of all lands, ethnic groups, and countries.

International trade agreements, as well as United Nation resolutions, have mandated that participating nations adopt measures to improve the lives of their citizens affected by disabilities. Consequently, there is often willingness, even eagerness, on the part of the governments of even closed and semi-closed nations to welcome organizations like Joni and Friends and evangelist, Nick Vujicic. These Luke 14 ministers, some empowered with wheelchairs, preach the Gospel and share the Good News with Muslims, Hindus and Communists. People affected by disabilities are mostly under 'the towel,' but definitely advancing God's Kingdom.

While still a fledgling, world-wide movement, disability ministry is growing like leaven, unseen yet with inevitability. By its very nature and the power of God within it, it is destined to infect the entire loaf of earth. Just as the leaven in bread dough grows, nothing can stop the process of God working in and through the mounds of people and nations that make up our world.

One day the entire civilized world will be affected by this exceptional leaven, and through them more of the world will be given the opportunity to feast on the matchless Bread of Life—Jesus, the Christ. [33]

Chapter Eight
Nick's Note

Mustard seeds and leaven. Here Jesus showcased a couple of the most obscure things in the natural world. Even though he had created it, Jesus was often preoccupied with the natural world. Perhaps more than being taken, he thought we should be taken by

[33] Mt. 24:14, Jn. 6:35, 51

what he created, and thus he pointed out the obscure and the obvious wonders of everyday nature.

You have probably read enough by now about Contagious Love and the Lost Mandate that you should be pondering what this all means for you, and contemplating how you should start taking action. Like making sure you are planted in the right place to grow.

You might think, well, I'm just this insignificant tiny seed of a person. People don't really take notice when I show up. You may even be a big guy, yet perhaps people don't take you seriously.

Remember, when that tiny micro mustard seed takes root in the ground, gets a little water, some weeding, and lots of abundant sunshine, it becomes the biggest plant in God's garden.

The Bible refers to the Church, to God's people as a vineyard. So plant yourself in a quality spiritual family, a Christian vineyard where the water of the Holy Spirit is available, where God's Word empowered by the Holy Spirit can weed around you and prune you, and where there is God's glory evident through worship and acts of love.

You'll be amazed at what God will grow you into. You'll be big in His eyes. The other plants will look up to you. When you are born again by God's Spirit, you are just a tiny shoot, but not for long. In a year you will be a growing, budding tree, and in a few years a massive tree full of life giving seed and fruit.

If we are honest with ourselves, we all are little seeds. Yet, God knows the full potential of what you can grow into.

Some churches have an eye for, or an attraction to, the seemingly insignificant people in their congregation. A church that recognizes and honors people with disabilities will have some of the largest plants of all in the Kingdom of God.

I ministered in a church of 20,000 once, and I didn't see a single place for a wheelchair. I asked the pastor what he thought about disability ministry in his church. His response was that they had talked about it, but nothing was ever done. Yet I have been to small churches where there are many people who have disabilities.

A church isn't measured in God's eyes by its numbers, but by the quality of its members.

- Chapter Nine -

A Tight Squeeze

Luke 13:22-30

After my first communion as a child in the Catholic Church, I thought a great deal about God and hungered for Him. I suppose I was around nine years old when I memorized the "Apostles Creed" along with the "Hail Mary" and "Our Father." During the winter of that year my heart so longed to know God that I prayed for up to three-quarters of an hour almost every night. I even had thoughts about becoming a priest. However, my desire to please God with those repetitious prayers did not bring me into a vital relationship with Him.

At fourteen years of age, after an attempt by a priest to have sex with me, and through my later youthful sins and rebellion (drinking, carousing along with marijuana and other drug use), I wandered from God, wondering if He even existed. I became agnostic and entered a life of narcissism.

Yet, I am convinced that God honored my desires and prayers as a young boy. I personally and powerfully encountered the Savior years later after saying an abbreviated sinner's prayer to a God, who, up to that time I wasn't sure even existed. I was marvelously and powerfully born-again by saying a simple and sincere, yet somewhat feeble and uncertain prayer of "God, I want you to come into my life."

So hard, yet it is so easy to know God personally. What was sincere, prayerful work as a third grader was no work at all as a sophomore in college. I discovered the reality of God through a simple sinner's prayer to a Savior who loved and sought me.

This Parable of the Narrow Door in Luke 13 reminds me about the early soul-seeking season of my life.

> *22 And He went through the cities and villages, teaching, and*
> *journeying toward Jerusalem. 23 Then one said to Him, "Lord, are*
> *there few who are saved?" And He said to them, 24 "Strive to enter*
> *through the narrow gate, for many, I say to you, will seek to enter*
> *and will not be able. 25 When once the Master of the house has*
> *risen up and shut the door, and you begin to stand outside and*
> *knock at the door, saying, 'Lord, Lord, open for us,' and He will*
> *answer and say to you, 'I do not know you, where you are from,' 26*
> *then you will begin to say, 'We ate and drank in Your presence, and*
> *You taught in our streets.' 27 But he will say, 'I tell you I do not*
> *know you, where you are from. Depart from me, all you workers of*
> *iniquity.' 28 There will be weeping and gnashing of teeth, when you*
> *see Abraham and Isaac and Jacob and all the prophets in the*
> *Kingdom of God, and yourselves thrust out. 29 They will come from*
> *the east and the west, from the north and the south, and sit down in*

the Kingdom of God. 30 And indeed there are last who will be first, and there are first who will be last.

"Lord, are there few who are saved?" This is a disturbing parable about the haves and have-nots. Anyone not made uneasy by this parable is in trouble. This passage, and its` parallel passages of John 10:7-18 and Matthew 7:13-14, tell us what salvation looks like, how it happens, who is in for the great and final banquet feast, and who is out.

The term *sit down* refers to being seated at a banquet in the Kingdom of God. Everyone's eternal destiny swivels on the truths of these bible texts. According to Luke 13:22-30, salvation looks and happens like this:

- It is done in earnest, because entrance to the great banquet feast has restrictions and requirements. It isn't easy. In fact it is impossible if we try to do it on our own terms.
- Jesus is the only way through whom entrance can be gained.
- It must be done in time. You can be too late.

In verse 24 we read *Strive to enter through the narrow gate, for many, I say to you, will seek to enter and will not be able.* Strive in the original language is *agonize*, the same basic word we transliterate from the Greek as *agonize*. This is a similar word to *agonia,* used by Christ during His suffering at Gethsemane (Lk. 22:44), and frequently used to describe those athletes, who in the ancient games (predecessors to the Olympics) earnestly and painfully contended to win the prize.

Let's be as clear as the scriptures are. We cannot earn our salvation by working hard or through good works. It is a gift from God that is received as we in faith trust Christ as our Lord and Savior. We read in Ephesians 2:8-10: *For by grace you have been saved through faith, and that not of yourselves; it is the gift of God, not of works, lest anyone should boast.* But the passage continues with the flip side of what salvation looks like: *For we are His workmanship, created in Christ Jesus for good works, which God prepared beforehand that we should walk in them.* The proof, or fruit, or sign of our salvation is known by our works born out of a genuine relationship with Christ.

It seems we have a dichotomy. It is agonizing work and yet a gift that can't be earned by works. A good number of Christians, like me, would have to say we agonized in our search for spiritual reality. We exerted energy, sometimes painfully so, by bumping into the walls, the gate frame, and the narrow gate itself, thinking it would open on our conditions, or the conditions that the many voices of religion and philosophy were telling us.

As I previously noted, in my late teens I walked away from Christianity as I understood it. I sought to find God or truth and spiritual reality in numerous directions. As a hippie and college student, I sought spiritual reality through psychedelic drugs, studying religions and various philosophies, only to find that the dark gateways I was groping through had only dead ends.

Free sex, drugs, and rock and roll didn't do it for me, and neither did intellectual pursuit, religions, or philosophies. From the outside it looked like I had it all together. I was a buttoned-up, hard-working (yes some hippies did work hard), honor student with a clownish sense of humor. I loved to laugh and make other people laugh. But in moments of truth with myself I was painfully aware that life was a bust if there was no reason for my existence.

As much as Epicureanism was appealing (eat, drink, and be merry, for tomorrow we die) it was equally empty, leading nowhere.

Life was illogical to me—living only to die. Logically, my two options were either that God exists, or that life is devoid of meaning and only death awaits us (nihilism). Dang it! Life appeared to be a fairly vacant proposition. So far I had seen no tangible evidence for the reality of God.

I clearly remember telling God, if he existed, as I walked away from Christianity, "God, if you are real and reveal yourself to me, I will serve you for the rest of my life, but I don't want any religious phony-baloney." Yes, I really prayed those exact words.

So, from the point of abandoning Christianity as the country western song goes, "I searched for love in all the wrong places." I kept searching, knocking on gates, and bumping into gates and gate frames.

It was about three years after that parting prayer in September of 1970, while driving with some former high school chums down the Columbia River Gorge, I met God in His reality. Early in the morning I popped a tab of acid, a psychedelic drug. It was a wild and carefree drive for most of the trip until I began to come down from my chemical high. In coming down from my acid trip I faced my same old, troubling dilemma—born to die. How can that be? What is it all about? I wrestled with these thoughts. I was bummed. This is the inevitable outcome of nihilism—despair. Nihilistic despair can only be sugar-coated by whatever pleasures can be partaken of in this life.

At about eight in the evening after dropping off our mutual friend, Jeff Campiche, at Lewis and Clark College in Portland, my friend Joe Doupé and I settled into sleeping bags in a travel trailer owned by his friends in Vancouver, Washington. It was an unusually cold September night for western Washington. I can remember seeing my breath as we talked. Joe was somehow different when we had hooked up for this trip. He wasn't using drugs any more, and he had a peace and contentment about him. I got curious. "Joe, what's going on in your life?"

His response was as stunning and simple as it would be sublime. "Jesus," He replied.

I was shocked. "Joe! Look, you went to your church, and I went to mine, and there were nice people there, but it was just religion."

He answered, "Danny, I'm not talking about church. I'm talking about Jesus Christ."

"What?"

Joe went on to explain to me Jesus's words about becoming born again. He explained it was a relationship with God through Christ and not a religion.

I knew He was speaking honestly with me. I thought to myself, "What he is saying is either true or false, yet I know He is sincere."

"How do I get Jesus like you got Him? What do I have to do?" I wanted the Jesus he found, which had so altered his life for the better.

"Do you believe you have done wrong, that you've sinned?" Joe asked.

"Well, of course. That's why I don't go to church. I don't want to be a hypocrite."

Joe added, "Do you believe Jesus is the Son of God?"

I thought out loud, "We'll, if he wasn't I don't know who would be."

At that moment, I learned later, God had given me the faith to believe, faith too, being a gift.

"Then just pray and ask Him to come into your heart," Joe said sort of matter-of-factly.

"WHAT!!? Just pray? How could that be?" I had prayed untold prayers as a young, faithful Catholic boy, and it hadn't worked then. Why would it work now?

"Yeah, man, just ask Him to come into your heart."

So I went into my logical mode thinking, "Okay. If I pray and ask Jesus to come into my heart and nothing happens, I haven't lost a thing. If I pray and ask Jesus to come into my heart and something happens, I have gained everything."

My prayer lasted only two words: "Lord, I." I had intended to pray, "Lord, I want you to come into my life." But before I could get to the word 'want,' the Holy Spirit rushed into my heart, and just like the scripture said, I was born again; marvelously, sublimely born anew by God in all His reality. I wept for some time, but not because I was sad or had feelings of remorse; no, not at all. I was totally swept off my intellectual, emotional, and spiritual feet by the power of God. Equally so, I was stunned. "God is real!" Jesus, the creator of the universe had moved from my questioning head to my heart with transforming power.

I turned to Joe with tears flowing down my face and told him, "Joe, I am going to be a pastor." I had no idea what a pastor was. My church tradition only knew clergy as priests.

Rising the next morning my first thought was to wonder if this thing that happened to me the night before was real or only a temporary experience. Perhaps it was an after-effect of my acid trip. But oh, it was real all right. Everything in me and around me was different. The grass was greener, the birds sang sweeter. I was ALIVE! Jesus, the angels in heaven, and I were having a party!

Contagious Love touched my soul in the greatest compassion connection of my life!

I tell you my journey-in-finding-God story because it is a clear example of what Jesus taught. It can be agonizing to find God in His reality as we bang into closed doors and darkened gateways. Once we find the right door knob and turn it to open the door, it is stunningly and marvelously simple, requiring only an uncomplicated prayer of faith.

Now, you may not have a "Star Spangled Banner" experience like mine. God doesn't come into everyone's life in such a dramatic manner. But we all come the same way—by simple faith in Christ. Your transformation may be gradual like a rheostat switch rather than a k-boom 450 watt light going to full power and beyond in an instant. But God's light is light however it comes into our lives. It is light (life) changing. It has the makings for parties.

Sure, life since that cold, miraculous, September night hasn't always been easy. In fact sometimes my experiences have been extraordinarily discouraging and painful as you have learned in reading my life's journey. But they have been with God rather than without Him. And that has made all the difference.

Back to point number 2: "Jesus is the only way through whom entrance can be gained." In Luke 18:25, we also read about the narrow door concept. *For it is easier for a camel to go through the eye of a needle than for a rich man to enter the Kingdom of*
God. - NKJV

The Greek word for needle (*trematos*) is just that—needle, as what one sews with. Jesus's point (No pun intended, but it's still a cool unintended pun!) is clear. There are all kinds of options, but only one narrow way to salvation, and that way is through faith in Christ.

> *Then Jesus said to them again, "Most assuredly, I say to you, I am the door of the sheep. All who ever came before Me are thieves and robbers, but the sheep did not hear them. I am the door. If anyone enters by Me, He will be saved, and will go in and out and find pasture."* - Jn. 10:7-9

> *Jesus said to him, "I am the way, the truth, and the life. No one comes to the Father except through Me."* - Jn. 14:6

Again, the Greek structure is clear. The word *"The"* represents exclusivity, *I am the only way, the only truth, the only life.* Furthermore, no one can come *To the Father except through Me.* Anyone else claiming to be the way is "a thief and a robber." It can't get any plainer than that.

Jesus would not be politically correct today. Yes, Jesus was exclusive. It is okay to be narrow about the narrow way if indeed it is *the only* way to gain access to the Father. This exclusivity is actually merciful. Jesus as God is making sure we get it right. Sure, this raises all sorts of understandable questions, like "What about people who have not had an opportunity to hear about Jesus?" My advice? Take it one step at a time. Enter into a relationship with Christ and let him as your teacher enlighten you. I've never had to compromise my intellectual integrity to become a follower of Jesus.

If anyone is truly objective in the study of ancient history and ancient manuscripts, one must conclude that Jesus existed in time and space and lived just as the Gospels say he lived. Thomas Cahill's *Desires of the Everlasting Hills: The World Before and After Jesus,* a scholarly and brilliant work, should put skepticism to rest in regards to Jesus's place in history. So the question is not if Jesus lived and died and rose again, the question is "What will each human being on the earth that comes to hear that truth do with that truth?" Believe or reject?

Christ's whole life on earth was about pointing the way and making the way clear. Like being lost in a forested mountain and a fellow hiker finds the trail. "Hey, I found the trail. It's over here." You wouldn't respond, "Don't be so narrow minded. There are many ways to get out of here without using the trail." No you would take the clear way to salvation.

The great Christian philosopher and apologist C.S. Lewis posited that either Christ was a liar, a lunatic, or He told the truth, and that there are no other logical options.

> *...I am trying here to prevent anyone saying the really foolish thing that people often say about Him, "I'm ready to accept Jesus as a great moral teacher, but I don't accept His claim to be God." That is the one thing we must not say. A man who was merely a man and said the sort of things Jesus said would not be a great moral teacher. He would either be a lunatic—on the level with the man who says He is a poached egg—or else He would be the Devil of Hell. You must make your choice. Either this man was, and is, the Son of God: or else a madman or something worse. You can shut Him up for a fool, you can spit at Him and kill Him as a demon; or you can fall at His feet and call Him Lord and God. But let us not come with any patronising nonsense about His being a great human teacher. He has not left that open to us. He did not intend to.* [34]

Jesus speaking plainly in saying he was exclusively the way to God, which some would call intolerant, is merely truth wrapped in compassion.

It's up to us to choose. If He told the truth, then the truth is He is THE *only* way to God.

---

[34] *Mere Christianity*, C.S. Lewis, Macmillan Publishing Co, New York, NY, 1952.

What truly makes this parable from Luke 13 troublesome is that these lost people actually thought they were on good terms with God for their eternal destinies, when they were actually not. *Then you will say, 'We ate and drank with you, and you taught in our streets.* Fast forward to the twenty-first century. "We talked about you, heard about you, admired you, and went to your church where they taught about you. We read books and watched documentaries and movies about you. Surely you know me. I know about you."

While seeking God must be done in earnest and can only be realized in and through Christ Jesus, we do have assurance of our eternal destinies if, in fact, we have come to God in the manner taught by Christ and the apostles.

> *So I say to you, ask, and it will be given to you; seek, and you will find; knock, and it will be opened to you.* - Lk. 11:9

> *That if you confess with your mouth the Lord Jesus and believe in your heart that God has raised Him from the dead, you will be saved. For with the heart one believes unto righteousness, and with the mouth confession is made unto salvation.* - Rm. 10:9,10

> *Behold, I stand at the door and knock. If anyone hears My voice and opens the door, I will come in to him and dine with him, and he with Me.* - Rev. 3:20

We know the way to salvation, the rite of passage to the Great Banquet Feast.

Don't put it off. If you sense God is speaking to your mind, nudging your heart, it is the best time to respond. God is initiating a direct conversation with you. Respond back appropriately. You may hear Jesus knocking at the door of your heart again (Rev. 3:20), yet none of us know for certain if our life will be beyond our next breath.

As a result of my powerful, life-changing conversion experience, I was a bold witness for Christ in my small logging, fishing, and tourism community, sometimes holding evangelistic meetings, even marching in parades for Jesus.

During one such meeting at a community hall, I had a group of friends from my Bible college share songs and testimonies of Christ's life-changing power. A former high school acquaintance of mine, Bryce, came into the meeting with some of his drug-dealing biker friends. As we worshipped and I shared my testimony, Bryce wept and wept. But when it came time to commit his life to Christ, Bryce wouldn't budge. It was as if he was chained to his chair. Indeed, he probably was chained, given the peer pressure of his fellow bikers.

Bryce continued a career of drug dealing and crime, eventually dying young of a heart problem, no doubt caused, at least in part, by abusing his body with chemicals. I prayed that Bryce would again hear Christ knocking at the door of his heart. And I hope in hearing that he lost those chains, coming to know the Savior.

Your parents' or spouse's relationship with Christ will not save you. God doesn't have any in-laws, grandkids, or stepchildren, only sons and daughters of His own.

Wouldn't you like to be assured a place at the Great Banquet Feast?

> *People will come from east and west and north and south, and will take their places at the feast in the Kingdom of God. Indeed there are those who are last who will be first, and first who will be last."*
> - Lk. 13:29, 30 (NIV)

You are one of those very people that God had in mind when Jesus spoke these words, "People will come from the east and west and north and south."

Come. Sit. Listen to Christ's words. Believe and then feast.

Chapter Nine
Nick's Note

This is my kind of chapter. Presenting the uncompromising truth about how a person gets to heaven. I'm an evangelist. It's my business to know how people get saved and to make sure I make the message of salvation truthful, clear, and compelling.

I know if I were to forget or neglect to present the entire truth, then people would probably not truly come to know God in a life changing, God empowering way.

There is one way to a genuine life changing relationship with God, and that is through and only through faith in and repentance to God through Jesus Christ.

And we must get the bad news before we can get the Good News. The bad news is we have all sinned and our good deeds, religions, beliefs, our philosophies, church life, or godly parents will not get us right with God. We have to each, individually and personally, admit we have sinned, and understand that God is just and will judge all sin and all sinful people. That's you and me.

But don't despair, mate. Here comes the Good News. If we will turn away from our sinful life and ask God to forgive our sins, he will forgive everything bad we've ever done, because he sent His only son to the cross to take our judgment for our sin. He will then empower us to live a life of purpose and meaning.

That's the only message that will get people's lives changed for the better by God and get us on our way to eternal life with God, while at the same time joining us up with millions upon millions of others who have become Christ followers.

The door is narrow, but once going through the door you will find yourself living in a broad and expansive place of freedom—freedom from fear, freedom from inadequacies, freedom from death, freedom from being a habitual sinner, freedom from disliking yourself and others.

- Chapter Ten -

A Relentless Love

Luke 13:31-35

My first love was Becky Wallace, a blond, sassy girl from Seaview, Washington. Becky owned my heart.

My love for her was relentless. After we dated for several months when I was a freshman, she broke up with me. I pined for her. I had trouble accepting the fact that her spurning was forever. I did all I could to be around her at school events. Upon reaching driving age I frequently drove by her house in my 1959 Chevy Bel Air. I sent her flowers. I talked with her friends to see if she was thinking about me at all. I was helplessly in love.

Our story from Luke 13 is about God's love, which is even more relentless than my 16-year-old attempts at winning Becky's heart.

31 On that very day some Pharisees came, saying to Him, "Get out and depart from here, for Herod wants to kill You." 32 And He said to them, "Go, tell that fox, 'Behold, I cast out demons and perform cures today and tomorrow, and the third day I shall be perfected.' 33 Nevertheless I must journey today, tomorrow, and the day following; for it cannot be that a prophet should perish outside of Jerusalem." 34 "O Jerusalem, Jerusalem, the one who kills the prophets and stones those who are sent to her! How often I wanted to gather your children together, as a hen gathers her brood under her wings, but you were not willing! 35 See! Your house is left to you desolate; and assuredly, I say to you, you shall not see Me until the time comes when you say, 'Blessed is He who comes in the name of the Lord!'"

On that very day some Pharisees came, saying to Him, 'Get out and depart from here, for Herod wants to kill You.' His enemies had figured out that perhaps Jesus was headed back towards Jerusalem, as indeed he was. Not only did they want to kill Him, they wanted to keep Him from going back to the capital of Judaism in order to limit His influence. *On that very day,* that is, the day when He taught the Parable of the Narrow Door. (13:22-30)

If they couldn't intimidate Jesus, perhaps invoking a threat in the name of Herod would deter Him. The son of Herod the Great, Herod Antipas, was a Roman-appointed dictator of Galilee and Perea from 4 BC until 39 AD. Like his father, he was vain, cruel, grossly immoral, superstitious, an egomaniac of the first degree, and the one who ordered the execution of John the Baptist. (Mtt. 14:10)

Greater yet than the hatred of the Sadducees, Pharisees, and Herodians was the love Christ had for Jerusalem and its people including the Sadducees, Pharisees, and Herodians. The love of God compelled Christ, in compassion for us, to His final earthly destination. His love was relentless. Jesus's reply to this death threat in the name of Herod went something like this: "I will continue my daily ministry as it always has been, and I will reach my goal to be crucified and to rise from the dead in ultimate triumph over evil."

> *And He said to them, "Go, tell that fox, 'Behold, I cast out demons and perform cures today and tomorrow, and the third day I shall be perfected.' 33 Nevertheless I must journey today, tomorrow, and the day following; for it cannot be that a prophet should perish outside of Jerusalem."*

As he stayed east of the Jordan River, and walked the country roads and paths of the Perean countryside, His heart was clearly in tune with and towards Jerusalem, the center of the worship of His Father, Jehovah God. And thus, the Master's heart began to pour out in love for the city and its people whose leaders were about to violently reject Him.

> *34 O Jerusalem, Jerusalem, the one who kills the prophets and stones those who are sent to her! How often I wanted to gather your children together, as a hen gathers her brood under her wings, but you were not willing!*

Hear the passion, the sorrow, the lament for the city—God's holy city and His chosen people. *O Jerusalem, O Jerusalem, the one who kills… How often I wanted to gather your children together…but you were not willing!* Throughout hundreds of years of pleading through the prophets and now through Christ, God sought His wayward Israel. What great love!

God is always willing to extend His love, mercy, and grace, and He relentlessly does so, regardless of what we have done, regardless of how many times we've sinned. He wants us completely whole and well in Him.

As sinners, before we came to Christ, we were His enemies. Now we are being saved by our previous enemy who is now our friend.

> *For since our friendship with God was restored by the death of His Son while we were still His enemies, we will certainly be saved through the life of His Son.* (NLT) - Rom. 5:10

> *If we confess our sins, He is faithful and just to forgive us our sins and to cleanse us from all unrighteousness.* - I Jn. 1:9

Chapter Ten
Nick's Note

One of the primary themes that runs through my ministry, especially as I speak to young people around the world, is that God deeply and personally loves everyone I speak to. It's the truth. As Dan'l stated, God's love is relentless for us.

What is more amazing is the power of God's love, which transforms life after life, once people of faith accept the fact God does indeed personally love them.

I am deeply touched when people tell me that no one has ever told them that they loved them. Like when I was preaching in Texas and a man came up to me and said, "I'm 41 years old and have cerebral palsy. This is the first time I heard that God loves me. And now I have peace with God about having a disability." Or the twenty-eight-year-old guy in Mexico who was paralyzed from the waist down from an accident, who after understanding the love of God for the first time said, "I can forgive the man who did this to me. Now I can get on with my life."

Powerful is God's love. Once it is received in the heart it flows into every crevice of our heart, mind, and life to transform… IF we allow His love to do so.

So be of good cheer. God personally loves you whether sinner or saint. (Little PS. Saints, Christians, are sinners, too. They are simply forgiven.)

Enjoy the fact He desperately and relentlessly loves you. There is never a sin He will not forgive (no matter how many times you commit it) and no prayer he will not answer.

You only need to believe and ask His love to rush to meet you and then receive it and thank Him for it.

- Chapter Eleven -

Guess Who Should be Coming to Dinner

"Guess Who's Coming to Dinner" was a breakthrough Academy Award winning film released in 1967 with such notables as Katharine Hepburn (who won best supporting actress for her role), Spencer Tracy, and Sidney Poitier. It was a breakthrough movie because it blazed the trail in Hollywood in breaking down racism, discrimination, and racial stereotypes.

The Bible has some movie-script-worthy stories embedded into it as well, packed with tales of intrigue and suspense. This one is loaded with drama as we come to center stage, to the premier event—Luke 14, the Luke 14 Mandate, the Great Banquet Feast. This has the makings of a John Grisham novel. Yet this story is a story of historical fact, not a novel, recorded by one of the ancient world's premier historians, Dr. Luke.

As we review this text, our minds should be pulled back to the beginning of our general context in Luke 13:10, the beginning of

Jesus's three month Perean Ministry. Here in Luke 14 the scenario is much the same—it is the Sabbath, and the legalistic, hate filled Pharisees are present, as is a person with a disabling condition.

> *Jesus went to eat in the house of a prominent Pharisee, He was being carefully watched.* - Lk. 14:1 (NIV)

The New King James version reads: *They watched Him closely.* They anticipated He would step out of line for they had set up the whole scenario. A. T. Robertson notes from the Greek text we learn the Pharisees "were themselves watching on the side (on the sly), watching insidiously, with evil intent."[35]

Sense the tension and drama. Eyes darting to and fro as friend and foe were wondering how it would all play out among whispers, snickers, scheming, and eyebrows lifted in disdain. Fear, excitement and anticipation were palpable. Once again, the Pharisees were convinced that this false messiah, Sabbath breaker, emissary of the devil would fall into their trap, and this time they would have Him. They would expose this impostor to the curious and those who passionately followed him.

Evil, especially religious evil, is, at its core, pathetically rotten, actually putrid. It is an insipid sickness that poisons the minds and hearts of people who are called to represent God and those that seek God. It's bad enough that they were being hypocritical (verses 5 and 6), and that they were attempting to stop God's goodness, mercy, and kindness in their tracks. Taking their depravity further, the Pharisees were so filled with jealousy and hatred for Christ,

---

[35] *Word Pictures of the New Testament*, Vo. II, Luke, A.T. Robertson, Broadman Press, 1930, p. 194

their hearts so hardened that they used as bait a man tormented with dropsy. This, a feeble attempt to trap Christ in the action of breaking the law by catching Him working as a physician on the Sabbath.

There in front of Him was a man suffering from dropsy. Suffering! Not just ill, but suffering. Dropsy is what doctor's today call edema; a debilitating swelling of the body, limbs, and/or organs. Often it is referred to as a crippling swelling of the ankles and legs, frequently caused by cirrhosis or congestive heart failure. It brought to this man a devastating weakness of body, probably accompanied with chronic pain and undoubtedly depression. This was a man with the shroud of death upon him as he struggled for each breath. He was helpless and hopeless.

Jesus was about to take their evil intent and turn it into good.

The Pharisees were confident that they would get this Jesus on charges of sacrilege. He would be exposed as a false teacher. They had set up the perfect scenario. They knew that even though it was the Sabbath, Jesus would once again not be able to resist working on the Sabbath as a physician.

A subplot of this scenario continued as others were jockeying for positions at the dinner table, awaiting a sumptuous feast, unconcerned about the man's afflicted state. They were hoping to be entertained by Jesus as they prepared to watch the Pharisees verbally joust with Him.

Warrior that he is, Jesus took the initiative forcefully as he bluntly addressed their thoughts and evil intentions.

> *And Jesus, answering, spoke to the lawyers and Pharisees, saying, "Is it lawful to heal on the Sabbath?"*

But they kept silent. The silence must have been deafening. The hustle, bustle, chatter, and murmuring ceased. Silence deafened the cacophony of dinner service clatter, laughter, and the buzz of conversations. Jesus had their attention. The uneasy silence intensified as He took this suffering soul *and healed him, and let him go.*

As in Luke 13:15-16, here He again exposes their hypocrisy (verse 5), for *They had nothing to say.* (v. 6) They were speechless. They simply had not the wherewithal to respond to the miracle and authoritative words of the teacher from Nazareth.

Christ wasn't done with them yet. His message was yet to be fully driven home.

> *Then He answered them, saying, 'Which of you, having a donkey or an ox that has fallen into a pit, will not immediately pull him out on the Sabbath day?' And they could not answer Him regarding these things. (vs. 5-6)*

Now Jesus had total command of the situation, and he intended to use it to lecture on how God's social and spiritual economy should look and what His kingdom should be and will be like. So, first He told a parable to teach about God's economy.

The Parable of the Pecking Order

> *7 So He told a parable to those who were invited, when He noted how they chose the best places, saying to them: 8 'When you are*

> *invited by anyone to a wedding feast, do not sit down in the best*
> *place, lest one more honorable than you be invited by him; 9 and he*
> *who invited you and him come and say to you, 'Give place to this*
> *man,' and then you begin with shame to take the lowest place. 10*
> *But when you are invited, go and sit down in the lowest place, so*
> *that when he who invited you comes he may say to you, 'Friend, go*
> *up higher.' Then you will have glory in the presence of those who sit*
> *at the table with you. 11 For whoever exalts himself will be*
> *humbled, and he who humbles himself will be exalted.*

This Parable of the Pecking Order, as I call it, was prompted by a common practice, which Jesus took note of. As humans most of us want to be near influential people, closely associated with people and places of power, prominence, and popularity. Most of us are drawn to power and popularity.

Seating at a feast in Israel in the first century was much like today's banquets where the host or person of honor sits in the center, the next person of honor sits to the host's right, the second most important person to his immediate left, and so on. People were picking what they thought to be the most opportunistic seats in the pecking order of prestige, resulting, of course, in discrimination.

The point of the Parable of the Pecking Order is a lesson about pride and humility, discrimination, and about who and what is really important in Christ's economy. In Christ's kingdom humility is hot. Pride and sought after prestige are not. The marginalized are in, and the self-important are out. If only the Pharisees, like the paralytic's friends in Mark 2:1-12, had compassion on this man affected by dropsy and took him to Jesus to be healed, rather than using him as a decoy in their twisted scheme. How different would have been the state of their souls and their eternal destinies!

> *12 Then He also said to him who invited Him, "When you give a dinner or a supper, do not ask your friends, your brothers, your relatives, nor rich neighbors, lest they also invite you back, and you be repaid. 13 But when you give a feast, invite the poor, the maimed, the lame, the blind. 14 And you will be blessed, because they cannot repay you; for you shall be repaid at the resurrection of the just."*

God's heart always reaches towards outsiders to bring them into His circle of friendship. When Jesus walked into a room, courtyard, or crowded street His heart and eyes sought out the obscure ones, the ones in the background, those at the back of the bus. And, as in this case, He always moves them to the front of God's attention.

Yes, it's the shut-in and the shut-out, the least and the last, the downtrodden and the downcast. God's Contagious Love and power are attracted to humility, meekness, and weakness. We see this throughout the Gospels and repeatedly in the Epistles. Remember *My power is made complete in weakness.* (2 Cor. 12:9) God's power is not fulfilled (or it doesn't find its ultimate and full purpose) until it interfaces with weakness. And the Church and you are supposed to be the compassion connectors of the two—*go out and compel the poor and the people affected by disability to come into my Church so it may be full.* (Lk.14:23, my paraphrase)

Churches like The Harbor church in Ventura, California, have their mission totally and completely focused on the poor, the disenfranchised, the homeless, and the forgotten, for which they are being persecuted by their neighbors and the City of Ventura. Why? For bringing 'those kinds of people' into their neighborhood.

With examples like The Harbor church, I have hope for the Church, that the Church will put aside anything religious contrary to the simplicity that is in Christ Jesus.

Our radical, counterculture Jesus is a minority in this hostile crowd and culture as He unleashes His counterculture message.

> I quote from Yancey's "A Living Stream in the Desert":
>
> "Recently I have been reading a historical study by Rodney Stark, *The Rise of Christianity*. A sociologist of religion, Stark investigated the success of the early Christian movement, which, starting from a few thousand followers, grew to encompass half the population of the Roman Empire in three centuries. In the midst of a hostile environment, the Christians simply acted on their beliefs. Going against the majority culture, they treated slaves as human beings, often liberating them, and elevated women to positions of leadership. When an epidemic hit their town, they stayed behind to nurse the sick. They refused to participate in such common practices as abortion and infanticide. They responded to persecution as martyrs, not as terrorists... Even their pagan critics had to acknowledge that early Christians loved their neighbors 'as if they were our own family.'"

It's taken an agnostic sociologist to accurately explain what makes the Christian faith and following Christ so attractive and powerful to believers and non-believers.

It should be no surprise then that we are commanded by God's word and exhorted by God's divine use of suffering to indeed embrace it, and embrace those whom it has crushed. Like rose petals crushed, releasing heavenly fragrance, this embracing attracts God to us. And thus it offers the sweet and enchanting fragrance of Christ through us to those who breathe and seek life.

The God of mercy always hastens His redeeming and redemptive love to the heart of the suffering. God's mercy rushes into the empty room of brokenness. His love leaps at the opportunity to kiss the hearts of the humble. His power fills the vacuum left by loss. And His plan is to use us to do this, as our lives and acts of love and mercy become the music which carries and puts garlands around the words of the preaching of the Gospel.

Tony Campolo tells of a time in his life when God used an apparently weak boy with special needs to start a revival at a junior high summer camp:

> "Everybody ought to be a counselor at junior high camp, just once. A junior high kid's concept of a good time is picking on people. And in this particular case, at this particular camp, there was a little boy who was suffering from cerebral palsy. His name was Billy. And they picked on him.
>
> "Oh, they picked on him. As He walked across the camp with his uncoordinated body they would line up and imitate his grotesque movements. I watched him one day as He was asking for direction. 'Which…way…is…the…craft…shop?' He stammered, his mouth contorting. And the boys

> mimicked in that awful same stammer. 'It's over… there…Billy.' And then they laughed at him. I was irate.
>
> "But my furor reached its highest pitch when, on Thursday morning, it was Billy's cabin's turn to give devotions. I wondered what would happen, because they had appointed Billy to be the speaker. I knew that they just wanted to get him up there to make fun of him. As He dragged his way to the front, you could hear the giggles rolling over the crowd. It took Billy almost five minutes to say six words. 'Jesus…loves…me…I… love…Jesus.'
>
> "When He finished, there was dead silence. I looked over my shoulder and saw junior high boys bawling all over the place. A revival broke out in that camp after Billy's short testimony. And as I travel all over the world, I find missionaries and preachers who say, 'Remember me? I was converted at that junior high camp.'
>
> "We counselors had tried everything to get those kids interested in Jesus. We even imported baseball players whose batting averages had gone up since they had started praying. But God chose not to use the superstars. He chose a kid with cerebral palsy to break the spirits of the haughty. He's that kind of a God." [36]

It is in this very manner that I believe God uses the suffering of others and ourselves to interrupt our false security about who we

[36] *Angel Behind the Rocking Chair*, Pam Vredevelt, Multnomah Books, Sisters, Oregon, 1997, pp. 163-164, as quoted from "Just a Kid with Cerebral Palsy," by Tony Campolo, U Magazine, April/May 1988.

think we are, what we think life is all about, and about what we think is important, or even possible or probable.

Suffering reveals who we actually are and what we are really made of, what we fear, and what we really need. It is our hearing aid, enabling us to hear clearly God's voice, speaking at full volume into our lives, piercing our veil of false security. Simply said, suffering gets our attention, and because of it God gets our attention, and because of that we get God's attention, and because of that people give us their attention.

Power without suffering will most certainly lead to pride. Suffering without God's power will lead to defeat. Both tools—power and suffering—are the essential tools of God, used to mold our lives into the Christ-likeness that He intends, and which the world so desperately needs to see and experience.

Luke 14:

> *...Then He said to him, "A certain man gave a great supper and invited many, 17 and sent his servant at supper time to say to those who were invited, 'Come, for all things are now ready.' 18 But they all with one accord began to make excuses. The first said to him, 'I have bought a piece of ground, and I must go and see it. I ask you to have me excused.' 19 And another said, 'I have bought five yoke of oxen, and I am going to test them. I ask you to have me excused.' 20 Still another said, 'I have married a wife, and therefore I cannot come.' 21 So that servant came and reported these things to his master. Then the master of the house, being angry, said to his servant, 'Go out quickly into the streets and lanes of the city, and bring in here the poor and the maimed and the lame and the blind.' 22 And the servant said, 'Master, it is done as you commanded, and still there is room' 23 Then the master said to the servant, 'Go*

> *out into the highways and hedges, and compel them to come in, that my house may be filled. 24 For I say to you that none of those men who were invited shall taste my supper.'*

At its core, this grand parable is essentially about the loving Father heart of God. The ethos of Christ and His Father are manifest in God's identification with us, to the least of us with His healing compassion when in our most needy state, when we are at our least.

In response, the invited guests all came up with excuses as to why they couldn't come to the banquet. Work, business, and personal relationships were more important than response to the call of God. (14:17-20)

God's reaction was anger—*Then the master of the house, being angry…* His immediate orders were, *"Go out quickly,"* and not just to the main thoroughfares in major cities and prominent places, but also to the *"alleys"* and *"country lanes"* to *"bring in the poor, the crippled, the blind and the lame."* (v. 21, NIV)

Let's pause for emphasis. Verse 21, along with verse 13, comprise a literal command from Jesus. It is not optional.

For those who think (and there are many) that this parable is only about the rejection of the Jewish leaders and the acceptance of the Gentiles into God's kingdom, they need to reread verses 12-14, which is Jesus's reason for and interpretation of the entire parable: To invite the poor and those affected by disabilities into our churches and our lives.

I firmly stand my ground with my stake driven deep that Jesus has commanded us to target the poor and people affected by disabilities with the Gospel in deed and in word. This is irrefutable. He said what He meant. We must obey.

Luke 14 is the only passage I know of in the Bible where we are commanded by God the Father to evangelism and mercy ministry with such intensity that it is recorded that He *became angry*. Angry, yes, because people refused the invitation, but angry also because of neglect of those with disabilities as the full text of Luke 14:7-24 reveals. They should have been invited by his servant in the first place. He was also angry because of the hardened religious spirits, minds, and hearts that opposed or resisted mercy to the marginalized, favoring their religion more than a relationship with God and with others.

This is no ordinary angry order. It is a call to battle stations and action! It is a wake-up and get-with-it shout. This is the greatest reason for action—the destiny of the souls of millions, even billions, of men, women, and children, especially those who are marginalized!

Waste no time. Go without delay. Understand that this mission to bring the lost into Christ's kingdom is of the highest importance. This directive for evangelism reveals more passion than any other ever recorded in scripture. God wants this done and wants it done now, without delay, with haste!

So…get with it!

This fervent order becomes all the more intense as we read in verse 23 that we are to *compel* or "make" people affected by disability and the poor come into his banquet hall and into the fellowship of believers. *Compel* comes from a Greek root word, which means to put your arm around a poor person, a person affected by a disability, and draw that someone to yourself. It means to hook your arm around their arm and pull them along with you.

In other words, grab the poor and people affected by disabilities, and make them come into God's house so that it will be filled, so it will be fulfilled in obedience to Christ's command.

In fact, many poor people would not feel worthy of coming into our churches. Furthermore, most people with disabilities cannot come to church on their own. They need assistance getting to the church or into the church due to transportation barriers and architectural, social, and spiritual barriers. It also means they are perhaps fearful of coming into the Church, as some churches have a reputation of being unwelcoming to individuals and families affected by disabilities.

Think of it! What if every church in the United States wrote out a strategic plan, and in that plan it made sure one of the main objectives was to ensure that 20 percent of the congregation was comprised of people affected by disabilities? What if every church in the world committed to the goal of 10 percent? What great witness! What great power! What great glory to God! What a party!

I am happy to report that the Evangelical Free Church of America indeed did take this matter of reaching those affected by disabilities as one of its primary objectives in its strategic plan.

Right on!

Chapter Eleven
Nick's Note

I love the story about Billy.

While constantly teased, Billy was undeterred. He was going to share his message all the while knowing people were ridiculing him. He made his way to the front amid giggles and taunts.

I had to learn that lesson after being constantly teased when about the same age as Billy.

Teasing and bullying are heartbreaking to me. I know its sting, its pain, and its lingering effects.

Like Billy, I also have learned the authority in proclaiming Jesus, how it overpowers all the negative forces that come against us.

I would guess that there is nary one person reading this book who at some time in his or her life hasn't experienced some kind of put down by another person.

Let's each of us be the salt and light that Jesus has called us to be, and courageously befriend those people around us who are ridiculed, teased, and taunted. Be a good listener. Hear his or her heart.

Let's get to know just one person like that, and upon coming to know him or her, affirm them in as many ways as possible.

- Chapter Twelve -

Discovering God's Beauty

Let's discover what's going on here in Luke 14 and why God is so passionate about people affected by disabilities.

I want you to stay with me here. Perhaps you aren't used to thoughtful teaching of God's word or depth in theology. You need to know that the study of theology is the study of God—it is discovery at its wonder-filled best. *We all need to see more clearly how beautiful God is, what a wonder Christ is,*[37] as He is the one we are to emulate.

Throughout the Old Testament we see repeated exhortations and commandments to care for and execute justice for the poor, the oppressed, the stranger, and the alien. Which gives rise to the question: "Why is the Old Testament replete with scriptures telling us how God hears the prayers and cries of the poor, the foreigner, and the oppressed?" There is a reason, a deep reason, why Jesus

[37] See *Beautiful Outlaw: Experiencing the Playful, Disruptive and Extravagant Personality of Jesus*, by John Eldredge, Faith Books, 2013.

primarily hung out with and ministered to the marginalized—the poor, people affected by disabilities, harlots, tax collectors, the country folk from Galilee, rough-talking ("Sons of Thunder" Mk. 3:17) and no doubt malodorous fishermen, even the tragic Judas Iscariot, the despised Samaritans, lepers, the ostracized shepherds—all shunned by the Judean "in crowd."

I suggest that a significant part of the theology (the heart and mind of God) here is Father God's personal and very strong identification with the marginalized and those who suffer *through* the experiences of His Son. Through His Son's incarnation, life, His sufferings, His life of rejection at the hands and hearts of mankind, His torture and crucifixion.

Keep in mind the Son of God experienced the following:

- Poverty (Lk. 2:22-23, His parents could only afford two doves at His consecration)
- homelessness *(nowhere to lay His head*, Lk. 9:58)
- a refugee (into Egypt)
- being relatively unattractive - Is. 53:2b
- rejection by family, community, and nation
- being misunderstood
- motivations maligned
- falsely accused
- falsely prosecuted
- falsely imprisoned
- falsely condemned to death
- extreme depression (the Garden suffering - Mk. 14:32-34)

- Fatherless, i.e., abandoned by His Father at the most critical juncture of His life on earth—*My God, my God, why have you forsaken me?* - Mtt. 27:46

Also keep in mind this is about God's experience in having a disability. Yes God in Christ became disabled for us:

- The all present, all powerful, all knowing God made Himself into the likeness of a man—severely (limiting) disabling Himself for us, to be with us, to be one of us, and for us to identify more intimately with Him.
- Voluntarily He went to the cross, beaten, humiliated, whipped nearly to death, and crucified under agonizing writhing pain. He allowed Himself to be literally pinned to a rough-hewn cross, and consequently totally disabled.

Jesus said, "I and my father are one." (Jn. 10:30) Whatever the Son experienced, so did the Father.

When I think of the affinity God has for those who suffer, my mind goes back to my life in the Siskiyou Mountains. In Southwest Oregon, the days of fall were cold and often wet. Here I was, pioneering my first church during the late 1970s. One morning I was in a hurry to get to an appointment, but didn't want to leave my family without some split wood for our wood stove.

Where I grew up in rural Washington State, like rural Oregon, splitting and stacking firewood was more than a chore. It was part of the rhythm of our lives. Nicely split and neatly stacked cords of firewood are somewhat of a status symbol in forested communities. It is taken quite seriously.

I was fairly well experienced at the fossil fuel art form of wood storage and consumption. I knew better than to take a light ax to try to split the local hardwood—Madrone. A heavy splitting mall should be used on such a formidable wood. But being in a hurry, I foolishly determined I was accomplished enough to split a gnarled hunk of hardwood with my light ax, just this one time.

Taking my first whack at this piece of Madrone, the light ax, as I knew was very possible, glanced off the hunk of hardened wood, slipped in my hands and entered my left leg about eight inches above the ankle, cutting flesh all the way to my fibula. Blood poured out. Pain followed. I hobbled to the house, and then with tourniquet in play, I told my wife that she would need to drive me to the local clinic.

It is odd what one thinks in situations like this. I thought these words, very logically, yet with a twinge of fear, "This is serious." Duhhh!

I made it to my 1951 Dodge pickup. My wife fired up the straight-six engine, and with our two daughters we began the eight mile trek down the two lane, country road to the local medical station (we were too remote to have a hospital). I calmly repeated to myself, "You're going to be okay, Dan. No need to go into shock. You'll make it just fine." My body was not listening to my mental exhortations, as I could sense the symptoms of shock beginning to course through my body.

It all ended up okay. I got stitched up, and I healed; well, sort of healed. There was residual pain for years. In fact up to 20 years later, whenever I drove by someone chopping wood, upon seeing them do so, my lower left leg would throb.

Let me suggest that it is no different with God the Father. As God walks with us in our pain and suffering, His leg (heart) throbs, too. It was His heart that was broken at Calvary. It was His son who was crushed. He totally identifies with us and demonstrated so through His Son.

Through His Son, God experienced paralyzing immobility, excruciating pain, heartbreak, poverty, extreme stress, abandonment, loneliness, distress, and even depression as He sweated drops of blood in the garden, revealing His agony of soul.

No wonder He is so compassionate!

Luke records Jesus, *And being in agony, He prayed more earnestly. Then His sweat became like great drops of blood falling down to the ground.* Matthew 26:38 (adds, *Then He said to them, 'My soul is exceedingly sorrowful, even to death. Stay here and watch with Me.'* The NIV translates this verse, *Then He said to them, 'My soul is overwhelmed with sorrow to the point of death. Stay here and keep watch with me.'* The King James Greek Lexicon defines this state of soul as "overcome with sorrow so much as to cause one's death." *The Message* reads, *This sorrow is crushing my life out.* Even God Himself thoroughly understands the pain of debilitating sorrow and depression.

Now that we have seen the reason behind God's impassioned motivation to exhort us to minister to the poor and people affected by disabilities, we are better prepared to look with more detail into a primary text of scripture regarding ministry to the suffering. This look-see will shed more light on God's heart for the marginalized. While we have already referred to Matthew 25 several times, let's look closer, peering a little more into the heart of God as best we can.

In the following passage, it is clear that God takes the treatment of the marginalized (or lack thereof) very, very personally. He personally feels their pain. Pay close attention to the words that I have underlined:

> *31 When the Son of Man comes in His glory, and all the holy angels with Him, then He will sit on the throne of His glory. 32 All the nations will be gathered before Him, and He will separate them one from another, as a shepherd divides his sheep from the goats. 33 And He will set the sheep on His right hand, but the goats on the left. 34 Then the King will say to those on His right hand, 'Come, you blessed of My Father, inherit the kingdom prepared for you from the foundation of the world: 35 for I was hungry and you gave Me food; I was thirsty and you gave Me drink; I was a stranger and you took Me in; 36 I was naked and you clothed Me; I was sick and you visited Me; I was in prison and you came to Me.' 37 Then the righteous will answer Him, saying, 'Lord, when did we see You hungry and feed You, or thirsty and give You drink? 38 When did we see You a stranger and take You in, or naked and clothe You? 39 Or when did we see You sick, or in prison, and come to You?' 40 And the King will answer and say to them, 'Assuredly, I say to you, inasmuch as you did it to one of the least of these My brethren, you did it to Me.' 41 Then He will also say to those on the left hand, 'Depart from Me, you cursed, into the everlasting fire prepared for the devil and his angels: 42 for I was hungry and you gave Me no food; I was thirsty and you gave Me no drink; 43 I was a stranger and you did not take Me in, naked and*

> *you did not clothe Me, sick and in prison and you did not visit Me.' 44 Then they also will answer Him, saying, 'Lord, when did we see You hungry or thirsty or a stranger or naked or sick or in prison, and did not minister to You?' 45 Then He will answer them, saying, 'Assuredly, I say to you, inasmuch as you did <u>not do it to</u> one of the <u>least of these</u>, you <u>did not do it to Me</u>.' 46 And these will go away into everlasting punishment, but the righteous into eternal life."* - Mtt. 25

Whatever we do to the least, we do to Christ. What we neglect to do for the least, we fail to do to Christ.

Some Bible translations render these personal pronouns with the preposition "for," as in "did it for me." But the better translation affirmed by numerous translations[38] should read you "did it to me" or "unto me."

The prepositional distinction is critical to understand. Jesus takes so seriously the way we treat, mistreat, or don't care for the unfortunate, the downtrodden, the marginalized that He tells us whatever we do to them, we have done personally to Him—not just for Him, but **to** Him.

A youth pastor who ministered with me at the Ilwaco Community Church, Marshall Snider, started a ministry for street people in Portland, Oregon, called Bridge Town. Marshall now trains young and old alike from around the country to do the same for their city's homeless population. Under the bridges of Portland, where the homeless seek shelter from inclement weather, homeless people are treated with dignity by the people of Bridge Town. Their hair is

---

[38] KJV, NKJV, NLT, ASV, NAS, RSV, Young's Literal, Rotterdam's Emphasized Bible, Douay-Rheims, and Weymouth.

washed, their hands and feet cleaned, they are fed, and in some cases clothed and given blankets. Now that is Jesus centered Matthew 25 ministry; that is His *Contagious Love* at work!

Perhaps many Christians, in seeking to discover more of Christ and to grow in Him, are not searching in all the right places. He is not found only in the Word, or only in prayer, or only in worship. And I don't want to understate how important the Word, prayer, and worship are regarding our relationship with Jesus. But, He can and should be personally ministered to and personally experienced in ministry to the poor, people affected by disabilities, and the rest of the marginalized. My experience and that of thousands of Christians will attest to the fact that in ministering to the marginalized, you will experience an aspect of the active working presence of God's grace in a life-changing way, which cannot be encountered under any other conditions.

Marshall can attest to that, as can his scores of volunteers.

Allow me to suggest that with a careful understanding of the prepositions used here, there is even more to be understood in this text. Before coming to minister at Joni and Friends, I had the privilege of serving the poorest of the poor in Central America and the Caribbean as a director at Food for the Poor. While proper doctrine or biblical truth cannot be based upon experience, experience can enlighten our understanding of truth as understood from God's Word. My experiences on the field gave me further personal understanding of Christ's presence with the poor. I have called this "Christ in the face of the poor," and later "Christ in a wheelchair."

It was the practice of Food for the Poor to take donors on what they called "pilgrimages." As a Protestant clergyman, I was comfortable with this typically Roman Catholic term because these journeys to places such as Haiti, Jamaica, and Nicaragua resulted in many people, even non-believers, experiencing Christ in a life-changing way. They went on a pilgrimage to visit the poor and found Jesus.

I continued to experience this special presence of Christ while volunteering at family retreats for Joni and Friends and ministering on a Wheels for the World outreach. When ministering to the poor or those affected by disabilities, the result is a special anointing of Christ or life-changing, working presence of Christ.

Most, if not all of those who have ministered to the poor and people affected by disabilities, have personally experienced Christ in a way they never had before. This is not emotionalism or hyper spirituality, but truly God at work, as the fruit of such ministry is Christ-likeness being formed in those who do the serving. It is ministry 'to' Him. He is intimately involved with us as we do so.

In 2013, I visited The Harbor Church in Ventura, California, a church that focuses on ministry to the homeless. I sat and talked to Roxanne, a lovely homeless person. Roxanne was a registered nurse who once had the typical two car garage home and life, but felt called to become a missionary to the homeless. As I listened to her story and that of her friend, I realized I was sitting at the feet of Jesus. This beautiful Christian had chosen homelessness to minister Christ to the homeless.

The testimonies I have heard of those who serve the marginalized all have a commonality. They go something like this: "I went to minister to others, and the table was turned on me. I ended up being the one ministered to."

Real Christianity in its raw and pure form is totally radical—it challenges everything in us and about us, and offers to transform us internally, spiritually, socially, and morally if we dare to become an active participant.

There are basically two ways to this intimacy of fellowship through suffering, in personally experiencing and knowing Christ:

1. Looking to Christ in your own suffering, and
2. In obedience to Christ, identifying with and ministering to those who are suffering.

"Shaya's Story" illustrates that simple yet profound decisions can turn disregard for the marginalized into triumph for all:

Where is God's Perfection?
Shaya's Story

> In Brooklyn, New York, Chush is a school that caters to children who have learning disabilities. Some children remain in Chush for their entire school career, while others are mainstreamed into conventional schools. At a Chush fundraising dinner, the father of a Chush child delivered a speech that would never be forgotten by any who attended. After extolling the school and its dedicated staff, he cried out, "Where is the perfection in my son, Shaya? Everything God does is done with perfection. But my child cannot understand

things as other children do. My child cannot remember facts and figures as other children do. Where is God's perfection?"

The audience was shocked by the question, pained by the father's anguish, and stilled by the piercing query.

"I believe," the father answered, "that when God brings a child like this into the world, the perfection that He seeks is in the way people react to this child."

He then told the following story about his son, Shaya:

"One afternoon Shaya and I walked past a park where some boys Shaya knew were playing baseball. Shaya asked, 'Do you think they will let me play?'

"I knew that my son was not at all athletic, and that most boys would not want him on their team. But I understood that if my son was chosen to play, it would give him a comfortable sense of belonging. I approached one of the boys in the field and asked if Shaya could play. The boy looked around for guidance from his teammates. Getting none, he took matters into his own hands and said, 'We are losing by six runs, and the game is in the eighth inning. I guess he can be on our team, and we'll try to put him up to bat in the ninth inning.'

"I was ecstatic as Shaya smiled broadly. Shaya was told to put on a glove and go out to play short center field. In the bottom of the eighth inning, Shaya's team scored a few runs, but was still behind by three. In the bottom of the ninth inning, Shaya's team scored again, and now with two outs and the bases loaded with the potential winning run on base, Shaya was scheduled to be up to bat.

"Would the team actually let Shaya bat at this juncture and give away their chance to win the game? Surprisingly, Shaya was given the bat. Everyone knew that it was all but impossible because he didn't even know how to hold the bat properly, let alone hit with it. However, as Shaya stepped up to the plate, the pitcher moved in a few steps to lob the ball in softly so he should at least be able to make contact. The first pitch came in; Shaya swung clumsily and missed.

"One of Shaya's teammates came up to him, and together they held the bat and faced the pitchers waiting for the next pitch. The pitcher again took a few steps forward to toss the ball softly toward Shaya. As the pitch came in, Shaya and his teammate swung at the ball. Together they hit a slow ground ball to the pitcher.

"The pitcher picked up the soft grounder and could easily have thrown the ball to the first baseman. Shaya would have been out, and that would have ended the game. Instead, the pitcher took the ball and threw it in a high arc to right field, far beyond reach of the first baseman.

"Everyone started yelling, 'Shaya, run to first. Run to first.'

"Never in his life had Shaya run to first. He scampered down the baseline wide-eyed and startled. By the time he reached first base, the right fielder had the ball. He could have thrown the ball to the second baseman who would tag out Shaya, who was still running. But the right fielder understood what the pitcher's intentions were, so he threw the ball high and far over the third baseman's head.

"Everyone yelled, 'Run to second, run to second!'

"Shaya ran towards second base as the runners ahead of him deliriously circled the bases towards home.

"As Shaya reached second base, the opposing short top ran to him, turned him in the direction of third base and shouted, 'Run to third!'

"As Shaya rounded third, the boys from both teams ran behind him screaming, 'Shaya, run home!'

"Shaya ran home, stepped on the plate, and all 18 boys lifted him on their shoulders, celebrating the hero, as he had just hit a grand slam and won the game for his team.

"That day," said the father softly, with tears now rolling down his face, "those 18 boys reached their level of God's perfection." [39]

Disability ministry comes with a cost. Doing the right thing, more often than not, bears a cost.

---

[39] The story was originally titled "BASEBALL HEROES," and was written by Rabbi Paysach Krohn, a public speaker and published author of inspirational stories and parables. Rabbi Krohn told Truth or Fiction.com that the story was absolutely true, and that he knew Shaya's father personally. (see www.breakthechain.org/exclusives/shaya.html)

Shaya's teammates paid a price by being willing to lose the game of selfishness, and in doing so they all won by being selfless.

Chapter Twelve
Nick's Note

I so relate to Shaya's story. I clearly remember—to this day, still with a bit of pain just to reinforce how real it was—how I hurt inside when boys and girls would not let me be a part of something they were doing just because I was different.

I worked hard at being accepted.

One of the ways I became accepted at school as a young lad was playing marbles. Because I simply was given the opportunity to play marbles, I worked hard at it and became famous as my school's 'marble king.' With just my drumstick I conquered the world of marbles!

The story of Shaya and his newly found fellow baseball players exemplifies how much we need people affected by disabilities, for that matter anyone who is different, to be part of our lives. As we do, the beauty of the human spirit, theirs and yours, is revealed as the wonder God intended it to be.

We become agents of God's restorative power and share in His favor as we partake of actions of love and hands-on compassion.

Few things are more poignant and beautiful than being the people of Matthew 25. We all become a part of Jesus and Jesus's active presence in what we do.

We are in a word 'transformed.'

- Chapter Thirteen -

Paying the Price

Luke 14:25-35

Beware! There is a high personal price tag in following Christ, especially in disability ministry. Compassion comes with a cost. The cost may be different for each of us, but it always involves sacrifice and sometimes suffering. Luke 14:25-35 brings this home.

Little did I know when I personally and marvelously met Christ in that travel trailer, on that cold September night in 1970, that following Him was going to be costly, extraordinarily so. Early on it was selling all, leaving the comfort of my relatives, friends, and a good job as a community newspaper editor to attend Bible college. Then it was years of long hours, working and studying, once again selling everything, including our car to finance a calling to establish a church in the Siskiyou Mountains of southern Oregon among hippies. There we lived in a hippie shack with no running water or electricity. We packed our water up a valley from a stream to our cabin where we heated water on a wood stove. It also was bit adventuresome and romantic, yet a bit scary and a lot of hard work.

Soon thereafter, we lost many close Christian friends upon exposing my sending church's pastor, who was also the president of the Bible college, for repeated infidelity and for purposely destroying the lives of those he had abused. I watched my former church and its related Bible college slide into full heresy and licentiousness. And then, worst of all, fifteen years later, I lost my marriage.

Don't get me wrong. There was a lot of joy and excitement in fulfilling ministry along the way. Serving Jesus is "life and life more abundantly." I have often thanked God for giving me a very rich and full life.

I trust by now I have made the case that there is an irrefutable command and clarion call to bring the Good News to the poor and people affected by disabilities, drawing them into our daily lives and the life of the Church.

So now it's time to think seriously about how we prepare ourselves, whether our mission is to love and befriend a neighbor boy who is affected by intellectual challenges, or to start a worldwide ministry.

Faithfulness to our Savior does come with a cost, and ministry to the poor and the people affected by disability, especially identification with them, often comes with significant sacrifice.

However, don't forget that in doing so, you will be obedient to Christ, you will discover newness in Him, and He will be more fully formed in you, summarized by Jesus's promise, "And you will be blessed." (Lk. 14:14) Let me add that to follow Christ in any and all ways comes with a price, but the benefits and rewards are sweet, very sweet on this side of heaven and eternally lasting as well.

Most of the training and mentoring (discipleship) Christ imparted to the apostles was preparing them for the price they would pay once He departed this earth. The scriptures describe the end game, the goal of discipleship in being a follower of Christ, and that is found in Acts 1 in His closing earthly directives. Here Jesus once again juxtaposes the dynamic of the tension of power and suffering in his final command to his followers after three-and–one-half years of training. "But you shall receive power when the Holy Spirit comes on you, and you shall be my witnesses…to the ends of the earth." (Acts 1:8, NIV)

The suffering part of the equation is found in the original Greek for the word 'witnesses,' which literally means 'martyrs.' "And you will be my martyrs." Not the suicide bomber kind. But the sacrificial, giving, loving kind. Albeit, most of the apostles were killed, martyred for their faith.

We clearly see by now, from the Gospels to the Book of Revelation, that in its real, raw, radically life-changing, world transforming form, Christianity can't have one without the other. Weakness and suffering are always coupled with power, and power must be married to weakness and suffering. Since the fall that is the way things have worked as He uses us to redeem mankind from the ravaging effects of sin and the work of Satan. It is Christ. It is Christianity. It involves a price, His ultimate price, and our best. It is what our lives should embody as His followers.

Remember, compassion is always action, and action always involves sacrifice.

The Apostle Paul said it this way, *Therefore, I urge you, brothers, in view of God's mercy, to offer your bodies as living* [underline emphasis mine] *sacrifices, holy and pleasing to God—this is your spiritual act of worship.* (Rom 12:1, NIV)

This greatest of commissions—Matthew Chapter 28—does not say go and make 'Christians.' Rather it commands us to make 'disciples.' Disciples are 'made,' they are not automatically so by becoming a Christian, or by simply expressing faith in Christ. So, ultimately we are called to be disciples.

Jesus set high standards for becoming His disciple: being willing to lay down your entire life, hopes, dreams, aspirations, energy, bodies, finances, and well-being, if necessary, for His sake. Too many Christians mistakenly believe that this lifestyle is for professional ministers or clergy. Not. We are all called to be disciples and to make disciples.

We read in Matthew 16:24, *Then Jesus said to His disciples, 'If anyone would come after me, He must deny himself and take up His cross and follow me.'* (NIV)

Just as it was in 30 AD, it is the same kind of people who are disciples, who are 'dreamers of the day,' who are world changers, cross-bearing, truth-proclaiming followers.

As believers in Christ, all of us should aspire to be true disciples.

Bob Deffinbaugh, in his teaching "Discipleship: Its Definitions and Dangers" (www.bible.org) says this:

> "Apart from His sacrificial work on the cross, the most significant thing our Lord did upon the earth was to make disciples. Our Lord had written no books, He had built no organization; there were no physical structures or monuments left to commemorate Him. He had placed the future of His earthly work entirely in the hands of His disciples. Had they failed their task, humanly speaking, the Church of Jesus Christ would not exist today…Who is a disciple of our Lord? Anyone who is deeply and personally committed to Jesus Christ by faith, who manifests the power and authority of our Lord, and who continues and extends His work."

The fuller theological concept of salvation involves a subsequent lifetime of service to Christ, where the act of salvation by Christ and the Holy Spirit is worked out in our lives, our actions, our thoughts and wills. Primarily, that comes with the sacrifice of dethroning self and enthroning Christ. It is a process, yet a clear goal for all who call Christ as Savior and Lord. As you have heard or read, *Christ is either Lord of all or He is not Lord at all!* [40]

So let's now jump into our Luke 14 text regarding denial and sacrifice for the sake of others.

> *25 Now great multitudes went with Him. And He turned and said to them, 26 "If anyone comes to Me and does not hate his father and*

---

[40] Hudson Taylor, quoted in *Hudson Taylor's Spiritual Secret* by Dr. & Mrs. Howard Taylor (Peabody, Massachusetts: Hendrickson Publishers, Inc. 2008) page 195.

> *mother, wife and children, brothers and sisters, yes, and his own life also, He cannot be My disciple. 27 And whoever does not bear his cross and come after Me cannot be My disciple… 33 So likewise, whoever of you does not forsake all that he has cannot be My disciple." 34 "Salt is good; but if the salt has lost its flavor, how shall it be seasoned? 35 It is neither fit for the land nor for the dunghill, but men throw it out. He who has ears to hear, let him hear!"* - Lk 14:25-27 33-35

Notice how quickly Jesus winnows out the multitudes following Him, separating wheat from the chaff (Lk. 3:17), true believers from believers of convenience; believers of the "loaves and the fishes" (Jn. 6:26), those who seek Christ for what they can get from Him rather than for what they can give to Him and for Him. The passage reads: *Great multitudes went with Him,* which is immediately followed by *"And He turned and said to them…*

In what He *said to them,* He made three primary requirements to be a true follower and disciple of Christ. He said that we cannot be His disciple:

- If we love ourselves or other humans, even family, more than we love Christ. (vs. 26)
- If we don't bear our own cross for the sake of Christ. Friends, that can mean hard labor and suffering. (vs. 27)
- If we are not willing to forsake all we have for Christ. (vs. 33)

His will is no less than a radical life for the God of the universe. It's the way he designed it to be. A radical life in the likeness of Christ is the kind of Christian and Church the world desperately needs to see. Such a follower of Christ and Church are indeed Christ's representatives that will attract a lukewarm and skeptical society as they see the God of compassion working through us.

Miraculous healings, feeding the five thousand, and walking on water resulted in huge crowds following Christ early in His ministry.[41] Yet, from the very beginning of His spectacular rise in popularity (Jn. 6:53-66), Jesus was clear about His message, even when it was unpopular. The twelve disciples were regularly confused, sometimes profoundly so, over Jesus saying things that were hard to take, puzzling, and even shocking.

We read in John 6:53, *Most assuredly, I say to you, unless you eat the flesh of the Son of Man and drink His blood, you have no life in you.* What?!

The reactions and results of such teachings were costly, at least in the eyes of those who count numbers*: Therefore many of His disciples, when they heard this, said, 'This is a hard saying; who can understand it?' From that time many of His disciples went back and walked with Him no more.* (Jn. 6:60, 66). That's a quick way to kill Church growth. Or is it?

Remember Bob Deffinbaugh's words: "He had placed the future of His earthly work entirely in the hands of His disciples."

The Master knew that the quality of a few exceptional disciples could make a far greater difference, actually a world of difference, than the mediocrity of many. Jesus wasn't raising crowds. He was raising men and women of God.

Many years ago I heard a story, from whom or where I can't recall. It's the story of a rancher and a farmer, and it goes something like this:

> *Farmer Fred and Rancher Rick had fields that abutted, and they would often stop after a long day's work and talk over the fence that separated their properties.*

---

[41] Jn. 2 - 6:24, Mt. 4:23 -14, Mk. 1:21-6.

Rancher Rick never required his boys to work regularly on his spread, giving them anything and everything they wanted, as Rancher Rick was wealthy, and thus, he paid hired hands to work his land and his cattle.

Farmer Fred always worked his boys, making them earn what they needed, and seeing to it that they didn't always get what they wanted.

At the end of a long hot summer day, seeing Farmer Fred's boys headed for the farmhouse—tired, sweaty and dirty—Rancher Rick could no longer help but ask his neighbor, "Fred, you are as wealthy if not more wealthy than I am. You don't need to work your boys so hard. In fact, you don't need to work them at all. You could give them everything they need and want. Why do you work them so hard?"

Squinting into the sun at his neighbor, kicking a clod of dirt with his well-worn boots, while adjusting his sweaty Stetson, Fred waved his calloused hand toward his grain fields and responded, "Rick, I ain't rais'n corn and wheat, I'm rais'n boys to be men."

Jesus is interested in raising disciples, not merely birthing Christians. He's after the mature produce once the seed has been germinated. He is looking for spiritual warriors.

Thus we read in 2 Chronicles 16:9 *For the eyes of the LORD range throughout the earth to strengthen those whose hearts are fully committed to Him.*

Friends, big crowds do not impress God. Large churches do not impress God. Numbers do not impress God. God is moved and deeply affected by hearts fully given to Him, hearts that truly seek to serve Him and others in the name of Christ, no matter what the cost. Being a true disciple is a state of heart.

Our Luke 14:25-35 story concludes with *He who has ears to hear, let him hear!*

The moral of the story is that if you cannot accept what Jesus is saying about true discipleship, you are not hearing; you're not willing to hear. And if you are not willing to hear and respond accordingly, you are not His disciple.

Sure you may be destined for heaven in trusting and believing in Christ as Savior. But what will you be once you graduate to heaven? Discover God's intended end product for you. Like Paul who wrote, "I have fought the good fight, I have finished the race, I have kept the faith." (II Tim. 4:7, NIV) God has designed a course, a race for each of us. Let's be determined to get into the race and finish it.

It's quality that counts, not quantity, when it comes to the Kingdom of God. And the seeming irony is that quality is what will result in larger quantities. Thus, it was Jesus's plan for twelve unlikely men, men He trained as true disciples, that since has resulted in Kingdom consequences of immeasurable proportions.

Chapter Thirteen
Nick's Note

In the Old Testament, in the Book of Genesis, we read of the story of Abraham and his nephew Lot. Each of their sheep herds was getting so large that the land couldn't support both. So Abraham gave Lot a choice of what land he would like to have—the easy grazing lowland or the tougher mountainous terrain. Lot took the easy way out—the lowland. But in that lowland was Sodom and Gomorrah—a dangerous place for a man of God. There Lot, his family and his goods were captured by an invading army. Later he was threatened by the evil men of Sodom, and was nearly destroyed when God's judgment fell on Sodom.

At age eight I thought I needed the easy way…begging God for arms and legs. But God convinced me at age fifteen I needed to live life the way God intended. If I hadn't said yes to the hard life, Father God's way, I believe God would have never used me to help over one-half-million people find heaven as their destiny.

As in the story retold by Dan'l, whose sons and daughters would you rather be—Farmer Fred or Rancher Rick? If we are truthful with ourselves, most of us would want to choose Rancher Rick—the easy, fun way of life. It's seemingly an easy choice, especially in comparison to a day's hard labor as Fred's kids—having to clean the horse stalls, buck hay, carry water, plow the fields, and get up at five o'clock in the morning …again and again.

Yet in your heart of hearts, after really thinking it through, I believe you would choose, after given a clear choice, Farmer Fred as your father. You know you would be a better person because of it.

Dan'l gets tough with us in the previous chapter. Actually, he's only the messenger of what Jesus is teaching, so don't shoot the messenger. I like Dan'l, in fact I love the bloke, and I want him around for a while.

Seriously though, this chapter is where your commitment level comes into question—whether you will join the rest of us who have sold out for Jesus and are spreading his Good News in Word and deed, or you'll join those on easy street.

My suggestion is that you pray, and pray in a serious heartfelt way to the Lord Jesus for yourself and your friends, family and fellow church members to give it up for Jesus and to be awesome dream makers. Yea, being faithful servants of sacrifice so others might experience His spiritual, social, and economic justice.

And in doing it you will have a life so full you'll wonder why you ever hesitated.

- Conclusion -

As Radical Dream Makers "Run"

> *Then the Lord answered me and said: "Write the vision and make it plain on tablets, That He may run who reads it. For the vision is yet for an appointed time; But at the end it will speak, and it will not lie. Though it tarries, wait for it; Because it will surely come, it will not tarry." Behold the proud, His soul is not upright in him; But the just shall live by his faith.* (Hab. 2:2-4)

So with faith in our hearts and the command to "go," we have a dream, a vision to fulfill, and an opportunity to be in the dream makers' hall of fame, radicalizing our faith, and in turn the Christian Faith, the Church, taking the Good News to a lukewarm, disbelieving world in need of the culture shock of the Luke 14 Mandate.

With contagious love we are called to be conduits of the life changing power of compassion.

The movie *Forest Gump* is my favorite movie of all time. If you've watched it you know that Forest is developmentally delayed. The story takes place from the 1950s through the 1970s as Forest grows from a boy into a man. He also had a physical disability, a condition in his legs that required him to wear cumbersome leg braces as a child.

A life-changing scene occurs as Forest, about 10 years of age, was being bullied by neighborhood boys who were throwing rocks at him. His friend Jenny yelled to him, "Run, Forest, run!" Forest did run, as if his life depended upon it, and as he did so, the braces began to fall apart, and then they fell off his legs altogether. Forest ran like the wind and never stopped running.

His legs, the simplicity of his heart, his kindness and trust in others, along with the providential care and provision of God took Forest through a life of trials, but he was also blessed with financial success. He eventually married Jenny, the love of his life, with whom he had his son, Forest Junior.

Metaphorically speaking, God is looking for people, people affected by disability, and the able bodied, who with simplicity of heart, kind and trusting hearts, will run without looking back, shaking off the shackles of the sins and weights that so easily weigh them down (Heb. 12:1), trusting in the grace and providential care and provision of God to be radicalized world changers.

Like Forest, we have astounding challenges in our way. We, too, like Forest are delayed, spiritually delayed. Yet, as Christ followers, we are called to take the Luke 14 Mandate and make it plain so others may join this fledgling worldwide disability movement; running like the wind with it, and going *quickly,* to *compel* the shut in and the shut out, the least, the last, and the lost, these one billion people, to discover the life changing love and power of God Himself.

Luke 14:12-24 is a vision from the heart of God to us, a vision and mission of inspired simplicity. It speaks of how He sees His kingdom—a time and place full of justice, mercy, and humility before God. (Micah 6:8) This modest book about the Lost Mandate—*Contagious Love*—I pray makes the vision plain for you, my friends.

We have indeed discovered the Lost Mandate. We have discovered Jesus to be in the most unlikely places. Now the Lost Mandate must be found in the sense that it becomes a significant part of the Great Commission as God's Word makes it—a focal point of the ministry of Jesus, and thus the Church and each of us.

The Mandate, therefore, must be a significant part of our prayers, our personal life, our ministry life, our church life, evangelism efforts, missions, and our time, talent, treasure and touch.

We must hurry and compel those affected by disability and the poor to come in. The fulfillment of the vision in Luke 14 is *appointed* for today. It *will not lie* for it is truth. It has come. It tarries no longer.

Without a doubt, ministry to the poor and those affected by disabilities has a prominent place as part of the compassionate power and presence of God—the blessings promised by Jesus.

Join God's dream team as dream makers and dream fulfillers. Become a dreamer of the day for your home, your neighborhood, your church, your friends, your community, your world.

The eternal, final banquet awaits us all.

On this mountain the Lord Almighty will prepare a feast of rich food for all peoples, a banquet of aged wine—the best of meats and the finest of wines. On this mountain He will destroy the shroud that enfolds all peoples, the sheet that covers all nations; He will swallow up death forever. The Sovereign Lord will wipe away the tears from all faces; He will remove the disgrace of His people from all the earth. The Lord has spoken. - Is. 25:6-8 (NIV)

About the Author

Dan'l C. Markham, author and consultant to non-profit ministries, has devoted his professional life to planting and growing churches and nonprofit Christian ministries. An ordained Baptist minister Dan'l served as Vice President of Development and Partner Relations with Life Without Limbs. Previous to Life Without Limbs, Rev. Markham ministered with Joni and Friends from 2001 to 2010, as Director of U.S. Field Services and then Managing Director of Field Services. He is now Community Partnerships Director at the Everett, WA Gospel Mission.

Markham has served as a nonprofit executive director, Washington State county commissioner, director at an international Christian relief organization and community newspaper news editor. He has authored numerous newspaper and journal articles and was a contributing author for Disability Advocacy Among Religious Organizations—Histories and Reflections.

Markham's first book The Cultic Phenomenon: A Revealing Look at Ourselves (Lion Publishing) covers the misuse and abuse of religious power. His other literary works include Man and the Sea (Midway Printery, 2013) covering the shipwrecks of the Columbia River Bar and its environs, known as the Graveyard of the Pacific.

Dan'l and his wife, Colette, reside at their restored logging camp cabin on Big Lake, WA. They have seven daughters and six grandchildren. Dan'l loves to laugh, make people laugh, speak, write and ride the open road on his motorcycle.

Addendum

The 33 Stars of Special Needs Ministry

33 can be seen as a tragic number or a number of limitless hope. It was at the age of 33 our Lord Jesus Christ was crucified. His crucifixion and resurrection culminated and crowned his earthly mission. It was from the Son of God completely broken and disabled on a cruel cross that confidence for the future was purchased for all of mankind. It was here that darkness was turned to light, where suffering is met head on with meaning and where death was vanquished, one for all and once for all. Take heart and hope from these 33 stars of disability ministry who are only a minor representation of the hundreds of agents of change, bringing not only ministry to people affected with disability but more importantly bringing people with disabilities to ministry to us all for the glory of God.

Ministry Stars

Nathaniel's Hope, Orlando, FL

Birthed from the inspiration of their special needs son Nathaniel, who graduated to heaven from the effects of multiple disabilities, Nathaniel's Hope and its founders Marie and Tim Kuck have built the nation's largest network of churches providing respite care for families of kids with special needs. They feature a one-day event every June in Orlando that draws over 10,000 people to promote disability awareness. http://www.nathanielshope.org

Joni and Friends, Agoura Hills, CA

Probably the most influential disability ministry in the world, founded by quadriplegic author and speaker Joni Eareckson Tada, Joni and Friends reaches millions annually through radio, television, publishing, social media and its Christian Institute on Disability. Their premier programs are Wheels for the World, Family Retreats, 25 US Field Offices and the Irresistible Church training program. http://www.joniandfriends.org

Key Ministry, Chagrin Falls, OH

Founded and led by Dr. Steve Grcevich, MD, Key Ministry aspires to help churches launch comprehensive initiatives to include kids with disabilities and their families into every area of ministry. Key Ministry comes alongside churches of all sizes when they have a child or family they're called to serve. The ministry provides free consultation services to pastors, church leaders and ministry volunteers along with training. It features access to Front Door online church services for individuals and families affected by disability. http://www.keyministry.org

Friendship Ministries, Grand Rapids, MI

Provides resources and curricula that celebrate the gifts of all God's people, as well as nurture faith formation, belonging and community. Its mission is to share God's love with all people, regardless of their abilities or disabilities and to enable them to become an active part of God's family. It's most recent project celebrates an inclusive adult Bible study called *Together* that provides learners of all abilities with an important set of tools so that each participant can grow in relationship with God and with one another. This new and innovative approach is designed to help congregations develop a sense of true belonging among people of all levels of ability. Through the use of interactive videos, Bible presentations, discussion prompts, and more, people with and without disabilities can grow in faith **TOGETHER**. http://friendship.org and http://togethersmallgroups.org

Christian Learning Center, Grand Rapids, MI

CLC Network, founded by Elizabeth Dombrowski, partners with schools, churches, and families to create inclusive communities for persons at all levels of ability and disability. As experts in inclusive education for more than twenty-five years, CLC comes alongside Christian communities to help them include and support all of God's people—regardless of their level of ability—so that the kingdom can be more complete. CLC's specialty is as a team of educational consultants and school psychologists who partners with Christian schools to help them meet the educational, socio-emotional, physical, and behavioral needs of students at all levels of ability and disability. https://www.clcnetwork.org

Mental Health Grace Alliance, Waco, TX

The mission of Mental Health Grace Alliance's (MHGA) is to *transform lives, faith communities, and society by building a mental health peer / lay-leader movement through support programs, education training, and collaboration.* Launched by a pastor Joe Padilla, married to a woman with bipolar disorder, and Baylor University Professor Matthew Stanford, MHGA conducts research in how the church responds to mental illness. MHGA is building a large network of churches in North America to offer church-based "Grace Groups" and other support to adults with mental illness. http://mentalhealthgracealliance.org

Building Behaviors Autism Center, Cleveland, OH

Building Behaviors Autism Center (BBAC) is an innovative non-profit launched by research psychologist Dr. Cara Marker from

Cleveland Clinic's Center for Autism to incorporate Biblical principles and teaching into evidence-based social skill training for kids with autism spectrum disorders. BBAC provides services to families of children with autism spectrum disorders, disruptive behavior disorders, and other special needs. All of its programs focus on treating the mental, physical, social, behavioral, and spiritual health of the child and family. With BBAC's home based and school based programs children and families have the opportunity to experience Christ's love through researched-based behavioral treatment programs, art activities, music, sports, health education, relationship building, camps and more. http://buildingbehaviors.apps-1and1.com

SNAPPIN' Ministries, Oconomowoc, WI

SNAPPIN' (Special Needs Parents Network) Ministry, founded by Barb Dittrich, has developed models for training parent advocates to come alongside families impacted by disability. Barb and friends have championed the needs of persons with chronic illness within the church while drawing others affected by chronic diseases to Christ and the church. With a life of trials Barb and her husband have faced extraordinary hurdles, not the least of which is giving birth to a and raising a son with hemophilia. She writes, "In our personal lives, we have seen God working mightily, giving us joy and confidence as we walk through never-ending trials. We have lived through joblessness 6 times in 16 years and other major struggles. But we want to share with others the blessing we have found in our lives: God IS the strength of our hearts and a VERY present help in times of trouble!" Barb is a stellar example on how so few with so little can accomplish so much for God and others. http://www.snappin.org

God Cares Ministry, Avon Lake, OH

A leading edge ministry for the infirm and institutionalized God Cares focuses on equipping churches to adopt long term care facilities and minister to their disabled patients, God Cares has recently launched a national initiative. Their goal is to have each church in American adopt one long-term care facility. The ministry provides written and video resources and offers churches and church conferences seminar training by founder and President Bill Goodrich. https://www.godcaresministry.com

Colleen Swindoll Thompson, Reframe Ministries (formerly Special Needs Ministry of Insight for Living and Stonebriar Church) Frisco, TX

Colleen is refreshing with a capital "R" as she writes of herself, "I'm…a recovering idealist; a witty, creative investigator of faith, a compassionate caregiver; a writer and speaker; and a survivor of a shipwrecked life. My passion is to help fellow survivors and life-strugglers steer through difficult circumstances and develop steadfast hope, so that they can navigate life with significance, meaning and purpose in God." And she does so with her speaking ministry and blog, robust website, host of her own radio program, books, and many more resources. http://reframingministries.iflblog.com

Debbie Kay, Hope for the Broken Hearted, Victorville, CA

With over 800,000 Facebook followers, Debbie Kay is a wrecking machine when it comes breaking down barriers to help others access hope, help and health. A mother of a special needs child and as someone with multiple auto-immune disorders Debbie Kay helps others confront and be victorious over pain and suffering. Hope for the Broken Hearted is a website offering resources, encouragement and scriptures pertaining to grief, death, divorce, abuse, illness & disability. Debbie Kay is an author/speaker/singer and a credentialed minister, who is certified in Grief Recovery and trained as a Life Coach. http://www.hopeforthebrokenhearted.com

Erik Carter, Ph.D., Professor, Vanderbilt University, Nashville TN

Professor in the Department of Special Education and a Vanderbilt Kennedy Center Investigator Dr. Carter is leading researcher and author on the impact of disability on families. His research and teaching focuses on evidence-based strategies for supporting access to general curriculum and promoting valued roles in school, work, and community settings for children and adults with intellectual disability, autism, and multiple disabilities. He is published widely and the author of *Including People with Disabilities in Faith Communities: A Guide for Service Providers, Families and Congregations*. http://peabody.vanderbilt.edu/bio/erik-carter

Jeff McNair, Ph.D., Professor, California Baptist University, Riverside, CA

A premier, strategic change agent Dr. McNair is a Professor of Education and Director of Cal Baptist's MA in Disability Studies. Jeff is a passionate advocate, teacher and yes preacher about people with disabilities, especially in regards to full inclusion of people with disabilities into the church. Author and Executive Director of National Association of Christians in Special Education he is Director of the Policy Center Department for the Christian Institute on Disability at Joni and Friends. http://www.jeffmcnair.us

Jeff and Becky Davidson, Rising Above Ministries, Cookeville, TN

Starting with humble beginnings and a simple desire to help other families affected by disability, God has blessed Jeff and Becky's passion and work, growing Rising Above Ministries from local to regional and now a national ministry robust with ideas, programs and resources. Rising Above Ministries focuses support for married couples of children with disabilities, holds worship services for families impacted by disability, including a support model for fathers of kids with special needs. https://risingaboveministries.org

Shellie Nichol, San Jose, CA

Shellie will fill any room with spiritual and emotional effervescence in spite of her experiencing life changing blows upon her emotionally and physically not the least of which is dealing with Multiple Sclerosis. Shellie and her husband Sundeep are adoptive parents and advocates for foster care kids. Shellie's always upbeat and meaningful broadcasts with Amazing Hope Radio brings life and hope into any situation. It is 24/7 hope refill station. http://fostercarechronicles.org

Matt Mooney, 99 Balloons, Fayetteville, AR

A champion of disability ministry in the US and overseas through film, 99 Balloons has the feel of disability awareness gone Millennial Generation. 99 Balloons powerfully communicates stories of persons and their families affected by disability while building inclusive communities so that every person with disability and their family can live a full life within relationships. 99 Balloons through visual art changes the story of disability by proclaiming the worth and image-bearing beauty of each and every human being. http://99balloons.org

Jolene Philo, Different Dream Parenting, Boone, IA

Special Ed teacher and disability ministry leader Jolene co-authored "Every Child Welcome". Dr. Stephen Grcevich, MD, President of Key Ministry, says that "Every Child Welcome" is the best how-to book on doing inclusive church ministry with kids. Jolene writes extensively and speaks to help the church more effectively serve persons who have experienced trauma. Different Dreams has expanded to support for dads and moms in the hospital with seriously or terminally ill kids, parents whose children live with mental disabilities or chronic illnesses, those supervising adult children with special needs, wives and husbands caring for spouses with disabilities and adult children caring for elderly parents. http://differentdream.com

Lisa Copen, Founder and CEO, Rest Ministries, San Diego, CA

Lisa Copen is a warrior, a special operator in the Kingdom of God who while suffering daily with her chronic illness and pain brings sonshine to all, routing out places of darkness, discouragement and hopelessness in hearts, minds and families impacted by pain and suffering. Rest exists to serve people who live with chronic illness or pain, and their families, by providing spiritual, emotional, relational, and practical support through a variety of programs and resources, including Hopekeepers groups, daily devotionals, book/gift store and the Sunroom online social network. http://restministries.com

Church Stars

Orchard View Alliance Church, Janesville, WI

Pastor Andy Stumbo and wife Ellen Stumbo and their church with modest means have huge hearts for and a major uplifting impact upon people affected by disability, especially kids. A majority of attendees/families at Orchard View Alliance are impacted by disability. Orchard View has respite services and offers two sensory rooms for kids. http://www.orchardviewalliance.org/get-connected

Saddleback Church, Lake Forest, CA

With its special needs ministry Super Kids/Super Teens and Bridges, programs that provide an environment that introduces biblical concepts.to young adults with cognitive and mental disabilities, the churches famous pastor and wife team, Kay and Pastor Rick Warren, have championed the cause of persons with mental illness. They host an annual conference that draws thousands to Southern California on mental illness and the church. Kay lectures on depression, grief and suicide. http://saddleback.com

Bay Presbyterian Church, Bay Village, OH

In addition to a buddy program for children affected by disability, church based respite for care providers and individualized Christian education, Bay Presbyterian has piloted "relational respite" in which small groups from the church support families impacted by disability with respite care in their homes and "organic" support. Bay also develops curriculum for the special needs ministry to align with content taught across other age groups in the church. They host a regional disability ministry conference. http://www.baypres.org/special-needs/?rq=special%20needs

Christ Fellowship, West Palm Beach, FL

Christ Fellowship (CF) coordinates training and education about available resources within CF and the West Palm Beach community while providing practical support. CF facilitates inclusion, accessibility and encouragement to individuals and families impacted by disabilities. They do this through programs such as its "Shadow" ministry, therapeutic horseback riding, wheelchair collection and distribution, art ministries, support groups and fellowship. http://gochristfellowship.com/support/special-needs

First Christian Church, Canton, OH

With age appropriate classes on Sunday for people affected by disability, an online church for those homebound, respite nights and a Jesus Prom for adults affected by disabilities, First Christian Church may be the only church with a pastor holding the title of "Pastor of Developmental Abilities", Pastor Ryan Wolfe. The church has mobilized advocates for adults in their community with intellectual disabilities and operates a publicly-funded day treatment programs for adults with developmental disabilities. http://fcccanton.com/disabilities-ministry

Brentwood Baptist Church, Brentwood, TN

A church within a church the Brentwood Baptist Deaf Church has its own hearing impaired chapel. Brentwood Baptist also offers special needs programs including buddies for youth and a respite program for care providers. http://brentwoodbaptist.com/ministries/deaf

Bayside Church, Roseville, CA

Bayside provides an array of special needs programs including weekly children and teen ministries, disability appropriate Sunday services, along with monthly and annual programs and events. Teen Harbor, a special place for teens with special needs includes social time, art, snacks, use of iPad with special apps, a devotional and prayer. http://granitebay.baysideonline.com/special-needs-ministries

First Church of the Nazarene, Pasadena, CA

Since "PazNaz", as it is affectionately called, launched its full blown disability ministry in the 2003 it has become a leader of churches reaching out to the disability community and a magnate to Christian leaders and churches seeking out how to develop their own effective special needs programs. Led by special needs Pastor Julie Keith,

PazNaz has a robust array of special needs programs and events including disability appropriate classes, a buddy system, respite, carnivals, concerts, ice cream events, summer camps, fund-raisers and conferences. Some fifty new families made PazNaz their home church the year following the 2003 launch. This major spurt of growth was a response to PazNaz opening up its facilities including a basketball gymnasium to the entire city. PazNaz may be the only church in the country that built a special needs playground for its city, in this case Pasadena. http://www.paznaz.org/index.php/special-needs/

Lakewood Church, Houston, TX

Noteworthy as being part of the largest church in the United States, special needs Pastor Craig Johnson, founder of Champions Club, has emerged as a leader and driving force as one of the most respected church-based special needs ministries in Texas. It is becoming well known across the US and around the world for helping churches set up Champions Clubs. Champions Club is a specially designed developmental area for kids, youth and adults with special needs. The goal has been to develop a program that would meet the developmental needs of children in four important ways—spiritually, intellectually, mentally and physically. The focus is on spiritual growth through God's Word, developing the intellect of each participant through the five senses, educationally through various learning tools, as well as engaging the child physically during active gross motor fun. Champions Clubs curriculum can be adapted to a secular school or public facility environment. https://www.lakewoodchurch.com/Pages/Ministry.aspx?mid=40

Centerpoint Church, Simi Valley, CA

Disability ministry need not be difficult. With over ten per cent of the church being people with disabilities this modestly sized

Southern Baptist Church under the view of the Ronald Reagan Presidential Library has no designated disability ministry. But the Centerpoint family innately has understood the secret of disability ministry is simply loving and individually caring for people affected by disability and fully including them in the life of the church. http://www.centerpointsv.com/

Calvary Community, Westlake Village, CA

This mega church north of Los Angeles has a simple mission of coming "alongside individuals and families impacted by disability so that they are welcomed and included in the services, programs and events at Calvary." Calvary provides a Buddy Program, Specials Needs Room, a monthly respite program for parents and other care providers along with a Sunday brunch fellowship for individuals and families affected by disability. The church campus has hosted the international Global Access Conference in partnership with Joni and Friends. http://calvarycc.org/special-needs

Bethlehem Baptist Church, Minneapolis, MN

It's not surprising that this stellar teaching church prefaces its special needs webpage with this from Pastor Jason Meyer: "We, the weak, welcome you to Bethlehem Baptist Church. The world uses a sliding scale that esteems the strong and scorns the weak, but the church values the weak because the church itself consists of the weak made strong only by grace. We are not a gathering of the self-sufficient." Bethlehem seems to not have missed one opportunity to minister to people affected with disability with a special needs nursery care, Sunday school inclusion, fellowship for adults with cognitive disabilities, support for moms of kids with disabilities, a disability section in the church's library, a buddy ministry, GriefShare and an array of special events and more! http://www.hopeingod.org/disability

Stonebriar Church, Frisco TX

The nationally acclaimed Pastor Chuck Swindoll and his daughter Colleen make an annual affair of a disability ministry Sunday—a worship day to learn and reflect upon what God has to teach us about and through the least, the last, the lost, the shut in and the shut out. Stonebriar believes everyone deserves an equal opportunity to worship, learn, and serve in church regardless of their abilities. Stonebriar provides a Special Needs Suite with classes for all ages affected by disability along with Mom of Special Needs Prayer Time, a buddy ministry, weekly painting class, a monthly life skills class, and volunteers who provide practical support to families affected by disability. http://www.stonebriar.org/need-help/assistance/special-needs/

Willow Creek, Crystal Lake, IL

With inclusion support, that is, the support of an individual buddy, students affected by disability can participate in the group settings of Promiseland (Ages 2-Grade 5), Elevate (Grades 6-8) and Impact (Grades 9-12). Throughout the year Special Friends events are organized to promote community within the church where families can have fun and meaningful social interaction as well as networking opportunities. Past events include bowling, Christmas, Valentine, and Easter parties, and a summer concert at Crystal Lake! Community Soon, a new program of Willow Creek, brings adults with special needs join together for community through sharing dinner, worship and Bible study. Social events and serving opportunities are planned throughout the year. http://www.willowcreek.org/en/connect/ministries/special-friends/south-barrington

McLean Bible Church, McLean, VA

In 1996 the church recognized a need to reach out to people with intellectual and physical disabilities, including parents and other family members of those children. What began as a Sunday school class of four children with various disabilities, has grown into what the church calls Access, a multifaceted array of ministries and activities that now serves more than 500 children and their families. Access programming includes Sunday school, parent support and training sessions, summer camp, sibling events and monthly respite care programs. McLean has been a leader in church based disability ministry for over fifteen years. https://www.mcleanbible.org/connect/access

47629805R00102

Made in the USA
San Bernardino, CA
04 April 2017